Surviving Your

Stupid,

Stupid

Decision

to Go to Grad School

ADAM RUBEN (PₕD!)

illustrated by darren philip

Surviving Your Stupid,

Stupid

Decision

to Go to Grad School

Broadway Books • New York

Published in the United States by Broadway Books, an imprint of the Crown Publishing Group, a division of Random House, Inc., New York.

www.crownpublishing.com

BROADWAY BOOKS and the Broadway Books colophon are trademarks of Random House, Inc.

Library of Congress Cataloging-in-Publication Data

Ruben, Adam.
    Surviving your stupid, stupid decision to go to grad school /
by Adam Ruben ; illustrated by Darren Philip. — 1st ed.

        p. cm.

    1. Education, Higher—Humor.   2. Graduate students—Humor.
3. Universities and colleges—Graduate work—Humor.   I. Title.

    PN6231.C6R83 2010

    818'.602—dc22

                        2009043371

ISBN 978-0-307-58944-6

Printed in the United States of America

DESIGN BY ELINA D. NUDELMAN

ILLUSTRATIONS BY DARREN PHILIP

10 9 8 7 6 5 4 3 2 1

First Edition

CONTENTS

1 / Stop? Drop? Enroll?

Many applicants believe that graduate school will be a wonderful land of chocolate daisies fed to playful otters in the
golden autumn sunshine under a prostitute-filled sky. Chapter 1 will shatter those illusions and, paradoxically, also provide advice to help you enroll.

2 / Selecting a Graduate Program

Graduate programs come in many miserable shapes and har-
rowing sizes, and now it's time to select which one you'd like
to financially devastate your future—in other words, chapter 2
will prepare you to eventually file for Chapter 11.

Contents

3 / Grad Student Life
You Weren't Going to Do Much with Your

In chapter 3, you will learn tips and tricks for your day-to-day life, including techniques for free food theft, alternatives to hygiene, and, given current stipend levels, the surprising nutritional value of sawdust.

4 / Research and Destroy

The purpose of research is to keep one's advisor happy. Or, to use a tired analogy, if a graduate student is a vibrator, research is the battery that fuels the vibrator, which sits in the rectum of one's advisor. Chapter 4 is dedicated to the fine art of keeping the batteries charged and the vibrator running.

5 / Undergraduates and You

It is with envy, resentment, and prurient lust that we regard our undergraduate colleagues. While we refine LexisNexis searches, they spend spring break in Mazatlán with twelve sorority sisters named Jen who "really shouldn't lick that, but, hey, it's spring break!" Chapter 5 details the proper relationship to maintain with undergraduates, an earnest rapport that blends disdain with sporadic boob-touching.

6 / Six Degrees of Exasperation
Law School, Business School, Medical School,

Graduate school can be considered the bastard step-cousin of its prodigal postgraduate relatives: law school, business school, and medical school. Chapter 6 is dedicated to the students who were dumb enough to stay in school but smart enough to study something that makes them employable. Fuckers.

7 / Let My Pupil Go

Finally, in chapter 7, the reader exits graduate school like a caterpillar gracefully emerging from some sort of shit-filled caterpillar trap. As an advanced degree recipient, you are now prepared to enter society armed with an acute method of determining, conclusively, whether your clients want fries with that.

FOREWORD

THERE exists a subculture of dedicated academics who view spending a decade masochistically overworked and under-appreciated as a laudable goal. They lead the lives of the impoverished, grade the exams of the whiny, and spend lonely nights in the library or laboratory pursuing a glowing truth that only six or seven people will ever care about. These people are grad students, and they are idiots.

This book is for readers considering or already committed to spending the best years of their lives without sunlight. You'll learn which departmental events have the best free food, what pranks to play on hot-but-vapid undergrads, how to convincingly fudge data, and why your friends who opted to take nondescript nine-to-five jobs after college were actually the smart ones.

PREFACE

SERIOUSLY? A foreword *and* a preface?

Yes. The existence of both sections can teach you a lot about grad school:

1. Much can be gained by stretching a small amount of content over multiple pages.

2. In general, such redundancy imparts powerful messages that are powerful.

3. Your reaction right now reveals whether you should be a grad student:

   a. Those unfit for grad school have skipped ahead, probably to a page with an illustration.

   b. Those who belong in grad school feel a compulsion to read every word (and, in some cases, to take notes and prepare an extensive critique on the book's use of dialectical assonance).

PROLOGUE

ALL right, now this is just insane. A prologue? Really? Are we stuck here in limbo, doomed never to begin the book?

Exactly. Now you're getting it. This book is like your life, and the prologue is grad school. You eagerly want to begin your life, but grad school stands in the way, and just when you think it's over—nope! Another section.

And the hell of it is, you could begin your life this moment. Really. You could skip to chapter 1 and begin reading the actual book. But out of obligation to the printed word, or out of inertia, or out of a misguided need to finish what you start, you'll keep reading and waiting.

A foreword, a preface, *and* a prologue. Ridiculous. I mean, seriously, what's next—an introduction?

INTRODUCTION

EVERY speech at my college graduation buzzed with a sense of finality. "You have completed your education," each one reminded us. "Now go contribute to society!"

And most of my classmates eagerly accepted the challenge, having known that this day—the official, robe-clad end of the beginning—would someday arrive. As they pocketed their diplomas, they envisioned their new jobs, their new responsibilities, their lives outside the academy. They entered college as children, but they exited on that hot June afternoon as citizens of the world.

Most of them. Not me.

And not all of my classmates, either. As guest speakers and valedictorians exhorted us to go forth into the real world, a few of us felt that the directive was a bit premature. We knew that college had ended, but we also knew that the "real" world was years away. We were prepared instead to enter a half-assed compromise between college and real life, a simultaneously intense and lackadaisical academic perdition called "grad school."

I felt a little like a cheater, like a twelve-year-old who still waded in the kiddie pool, knowing it was well past time to start swimming, but was frightened of the loud teenagers in the big pool. Or maybe like a budding musician who'd mastered Guitar Hero, but had never picked up an actual guitar.

Instead of a job and a boss and a mortgage, September would bring another college campus with its dorms and quads and classrooms—and we wouldn't even feel like its most welcome occupants.

We would walk around our new planned communities in a daze, not quite fitting in with the social culture, and not really supposed to. We would experience all the disorientation of a new campus—just as we did four years before—but none of the excitement. And we'd have no idea whether to go to the football games.

I spent the first two months of grad school determining whether three amino acid residues (out of hundreds) were important for the functioning of a certain protein (out of thousands) that helps certain bacteria eat a sugar called arabinose.

I demonstrated that those three residues are not important.

Two months.

But that's grad school. You take a tiny corner of the universe that a professor finds fascinating and bury your face in it, looking up only occasionally to steal unattended bagels.

At the end of two months, I felt ready to announce my discovery to the world. "Residues 103, 107, and 109 are unimportant!" I wanted to cry from the hilltops. "Unimportant!" But a journal article never quite coalesced, and I moved on to a different lab, and now exactly zero people know about my discovery—which, had I ended up publishing the results, would have been exactly the number of people who cared.

What *was* this? Throughout my life, I felt I was gearing up to *do* something. Now I had finished my college education, and as a reward, I got to sit in an ignored corner of an academic building, growing and harvesting plate after plate of meaningless bacteria, solely for the sake of turning grant money into PowerPoint slides into fodder for more grant money.

To a member of the generation that was reminded at

every turn, "You're special!" nothing strikes a blow like realizing you've reached adulthood positioned to be completely, maybe permanently, irrelevant.

Hence this book. No matter where you are in the grad school process, you've probably felt this way (or will soon).

Sure, you love what you study—but to the exclusion of nearly all else? When you're typing page three of a twenty-five-page paper at 4:00 a.m., sucking down your ninth Red Bull of the night, will you honestly feel there's nothing you'd rather do? Or will you shut your laptop in anger, thrust your head into your hands, and lament your stupid, stupid decision to go to grad school?

If there's one thing I've learned from writing a book about grad school, it's that writing a book about college must be easy. Most college students are young and overconfident; they drink beer, go to classes, take exams, write papers, party, live in dorms, and deal with professors, parents, and roommates—in other words, their experiences are relatively universal.

Grad students are all different. You could earn a master's, a PhD, a JD, an MBA, a DVM, (that's a Doctor of Veterinary Medicine), or one of hundreds of other degrees. Your daily routine could include hours of classroom instruction (either giving or receiving it), or you may never need to attend class. You might obligatorily spend twelve hours a day in a lab, or you might have to research your dissertation at your own pace in a location of your choosing. Hell, you may not even write a dissertation. You also might not have oral exams, teaching responsibilities, or an actual advisor. Your program may stop after a flat-out guaranteed two years, or you could find yourself puttering around campus a decade later, swearing up and down that you're going to graduate any minute. You might be twenty-two years old and eager to spend the rest of your life studying particle physics, or you might be fifty, have a job and a family, and have decided to earn an MBA at night online for a little salary bump.

So here's what I don't want. I don't want to find my book on Amazon.com with little user reviews that say things like this:

★☆☆☆☆ **What the hell is a "thesis"?** April 13, 2010
By **Stupid Whiny Complainer**
Not everything in this book applied to me! Waah! Waah!

If you read a sentence in this book about the GRE, for example, and you're getting your advanced degree from a pharmacy college, which means you've taken the PCAT instead—let it go. As grad school teaches in spades, it's not all about you. In fact, almost nothing is.

So relax, enjoy, and please fight the urge to take notes. Maybe you'll even learn something, which is allegedly the point of grad school.

Then get back to work.

Surviving Your

Stupid,

Stupid

Decision

to Go to Grad School

1

Stop? Drop? Enroll?

DECIDING WHETHER TO RUIN YOUR LIFE

WHEN facing a major decision—say, whether to buy a car—take a piece of paper and make two columns. Label one "Pros" and the other "Cons." In these columns, write the positive and negative factors that will influence your decision. (For example, "On the one hand, I'd have an easier commute, but on the other hand, I'd have to pay for parking.") Then see which list is longer—and your decision is made.

When deciding whether to go to grad school, the process is similar. Take a piece of paper and make two columns. Label one "Cons" and the other "Super Cons." In these columns, write the negative and *really* negative factors that influence your decision. (For example, "On the one hand, I'd feel overworked, but on the other hand, I'd also be depressed.") Then see which list is longer—and do whatever the hell you want anyway.

After all, the decision to attend grad school is made with

the heart, not with the head. And your heart is a moron. Your heart says, "I love to learn!" while your head says, "Hey, wait a minute. I'm the one who has to do the learning!"

But you can't fight an organ that could kill you at any moment, so listen to your heart. If it says, "Go to grad school," you know what to do. (See a doctor. It's supposed to say, "Ka-thump, ka-thump." Seriously. If your heart speaks words, you're fucked.)

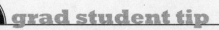

grad student tip

Grad school would seem exactly like purgatory if it weren't so much like hell.

Two Schools of Thought

Some people think grad school will be just like another few years of college: "College was fun, so grad school will be even funner, because I'll be able to buy alcohol legally!" These are typically the same people who don't see anything wrong with the word *funner*.

In reality, graduate school can be considered an extension of college in the same way that death can be considered an extension of life.

Some of the primary differences between college and grad school:

2

	In College	In Grad School
You drink coffee . . .	on Monday mornings to recover from hangovers.	four or five times a day to keep yourself, at best, in a semi-lucid state called "autopilot."
The absolute highlight of every week is . . .	Friday night, when you can stay out late and have fun with good friends and cheap booze.	Wednesday afternoon, when your department has a seminar that includes free doughnuts.
A "union" is . . .	the place where students hang out, eat, and play pool.	something you and your fellow graduate laborers are not allowed to form.
You drink away . . .	the night.	your sorrows.
You're upset because the clerk at the local convenience store . . .	starts carding.	makes more money than you.
You study because . . .	you have to.	you *want* to. Holy shit.
You sometimes neglect your work because . . .	you're going to parties, socializing, and enjoying your newfound freedom.	you're doing other work.
You're excited because you just successfully hooked up . . .	with this really hot guy or girl you've had your eye on.	your laptop to the library server.
You live in . . .	a small, cramped, sub-standard box called a "dorm."	a small, cramped, substandard box called a "studio apartment."
Sometimes, as an accessory, you wear . . .	a pledge pin.	a USB flash drive.
You find this table . . .	amusing.	depressing.

Quiz: Is Grad School Right for Me? Or Do I Prefer Joy?

Stop! Before you decide to matriculate, which is a hilarious word, consider that grad school is not for everyone. For example, supermodels can count themselves out right away, as can regular models, athletes, aesthetes, optimists, social butterflies, the "in" crowd, the outward bound, the upwardly mobile, international singing sensations, aristocracy, the generally well-adjusted, and anyone else already enjoying life.

To determine whether grad school is right for you, take this simple quiz. (Hint: If you're reading this book for pleasure but thinking, "Hooray! I get to take a quiz!," you're halfway there.)

Here's a criterion to start you off. This quiz is like the ones you see in *Glamour* or *Cosmo*. If when you see those titles, you picture them in your mind like this...

Glamour: (J Glam **6**(23): 13826-8)

Cosmo: (Cos Rev Lett B **167**(1): 220-9)

... you're ready to enroll.

1. I want my significant other to
    a. love me forever!
    b. stick with me through good times and bad!
    c. abandon me after two or three frustrating years of incompatible schedules.

2. To me, money is
    a. very important.
    b. somewhat important.
    c. wholly unnecessary and loathsome. Fie upon thee, o vile money!

3. **If I were an animal, I would be**

   a. a tiger.

   b. a bear.

   c. a tiger or a bear who is in grad school.

4. **At least half my conversations include the phrase**

   a. "It was the best time I've had in my entire life."

   b. "It was the drunkest I've ever been, *ever.*"

   c. "It was one of the more thoughtful pieces I've heard on NPR this week."

5. **The most beautiful thing in the world is**

   a. a rainbow.

   b. true love.

   c. the Euler equation.

6. When I was little, I always wanted to be

    a. an astronaut.

    b. the President.

    c. someone who designs a small valve on an astronaut's shoe or publishes esoteric analyses of presidential policy.

7. I see a tray of free pastries. I think,

    a. "These look pretty good. I may eat one."

    b. "I'm not very hungry. Oh well."

    c. "Well, that takes care of this week's breakfasts, lunches, and dinners."

8. I'd love to earn fame and notoriety

    a. right now!

    b. during a long and successful career.

    c. for someone else.

9. Train A leaves New York at 9:03 a.m. traveling at 80 miles per hour, and Train B leaves Washington, D.C., at 10:18 a.m. traveling at 70 miles per hour. If both trains maintain a constant speed,

    a. Train A will have traveled 100 miles by the time Train B departs.

    b. the two trains will pass each other near Wilmington, Delaware.

    c. I can still only afford the Chinatown bus.

10. I hope

    a. someday to achieve greatness.

    b. for a secure, stable future.

    c. rarely.

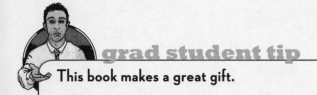

If you answered "a" or "b" to most questions, relax! Enjoy yourself! You have a rich and rewarding life ahead of you, no part of which should be spent in academia. Go directly to the frat house.

If you answered "c" to most questions, fuck. You're perfect for grad school. Say goodbye to your social life, your finances, and any friends who don't study the same subject.

Grad Libs

When you're a kid, Mad Libs are silly. You bought a <u>duck</u> in <u>Florida</u> and carried it <u>greasily</u>? Ha ha ha! Children are easily amused because children are dumb.

Then you graduate to the adolescent world of Mad Libs, in which you make every filled-in blank a dirty word, regardless of whether a dirty word exists for that part of speech. For example, you might write that you bought a <u>wiener</u> in <u>Butt Land</u> and carried it <u>boobily</u>. You learn soon enough that the list of smutty adverbs is a mighty short list, and there's only one filthy conjunction: *but*.

Now you're too old for Mad Libs. You've matured. You've moved on.

It's time for Grad Libs.

A Typical Day in Grad School

Today I woke up at_____. I felt very_____! Since my big
ungodly hour   *dismal adjective*

_____was due at_____, I decided I would eat a quick_____
horrifying academic *absurdly soon time*   *food nearest*
project   *your hands*

and get to work.

However, no sooner had I arranged my_____ in my _____,
implements of scholarly   *insufficient campus*
awesomeness   *space*

than a knock came at the_____. It was_____, who wanted to
knockable noun   *name of suck-up*
grad student in your
department

bug me about founding a _____.
name of useless organization you don't
have time for, such as a journal club

Scared that I might not finish my project on time, I distracted

_____. "Oh look!" I exclaimed, pointing down the hall. "Is
name of suck-up

that_____? You should ask him about his research!" Thankfully,
name of tenured professor who
enjoys having smoke blown up his ass

_____ ran off, and I got back to work—but then another knock came
name of suck-up

at the _____! This time it was _____, one of my students
same knockable noun   *name of shitty undergrad*

in_____. "_____," the student_____. "_____!"
name of shitty *annoying question*   *whiny past-*   *litany of unlikely*
class   *about recent exam*   *tense verb*   *excuses conveying*
                                                           sense of entitlement

Feeling a tiny bit_____, I called the student a _____and
adjective that means   *noun that rhymes*
VERY STRESSED OUT   *with "other trucker"*

instructed the student to_____.
action involving
interior body part

(As a result, next week I have an appointment with _____.)

name of academic disciplinary body

With only _____ minutes left to work on my project, I tried to

scarily tiny number

concentrate—but a third knock came at the _____!

Door. The knockable noun is "door."

It was my advisor, looking _____. Breathing fire out of her

adjective that means the opposite of "delighted"

_____, she demanded to see a draft of my _____.

I don't know, pick a body part   oh God, this word is going to be "dissertation," isn't it?

I lied and said I'd have something to show her at _____,

literally impossible time

and she looked disappointed and reminded me that I'll never be as good as

_____.

name of other grad student your advisor always compares you to

My advisor is an _____.

asshole

Then I looked at the clock and noticed I had run out of time! I would never

finish the big _____, never receive my _____, never

horrifying academic project   coveted degree

justify my _____, _____ decision to go to grad school.

adjective   adjective

Then my alarm clock rang. Thank goodness it was all a dream! The big

_____ was due weeks ago.

horrifying academic project

Blockin' Out the Scenery, Breakin' My Mind

Still not sure if you should go to grad school? Look for the top ten signs that you belong in an institution (pause) of higher learning:

10. You have friends who got high-paying jobs doing something easy right out of college . . . and for some reason, you don't envy them.

9. You could talk for hours about the awesome features in the new versions of EndNote or RefWorks.

8. No one depends on you financially.

7. In college, your favorite classes were the most fascinating ones, not the easiest ones. And you did all the "optional" reading—and loved it.

6. You find yourself describing academic texts using the same terms other people use to describe extreme sports. ("That gnarly textbook chapter by Hoffman et al. is such an adrenaline rush that it rocks the fucking universe!")

5. You think the job market will improve in a generation or so, right when you'll be ready to join it.

grad student tip

Genetically, if you marry another grad student, your children will also be grad students. It's true. You can draw the Punnett square.

4. You feel a deep love for a particular citation style and genuine contempt for all other citation styles.

3. It's been too long since you had a good bout of nervous diarrhea.

2. To you, "semiformal" attire means wearing a T-shirt that wasn't free.

And the number one sign you should go to grad school:

1. Despite all you've just learned, you still freaking want to. That's the only sign you'll heed, anyway.

grad student tip

If you have kids while you're in grad school, I'm calling Child Services.

Making Cents

Before committing to your program, ask yourself two basic questions: Can you afford to go to grad school? And if you can't, will that stop you?

Write the annual amounts you're likely to receive from the following sources on the blank lines. Add them. If the final total is less than the cost of your graduate program, but you still want to enroll, consider sleeping with a lonely financial aid officer.

grad student tip

It just doesn't matter.

Departmental Aid

In some programs, your department may actually give you an annual stipend or fellowship. To calculate the amount they're likely to offer, look up the average cost of living in your area and divide by a thousand while cackling maniacally. _____

Research Assistantship

If you take an RA position, you'll perform cutting-edge studies using state-of-the-art equipment and get your name in prestigious publications, giving you a leg up for the rest of your career. Just kidding. You'll wash glassware. _____

Teaching Assistantship

When you're in college, the TAs seem like aliens—a species of students slightly too old to be your friends, who probably live in the academic building where they proctor your exams. This is only mostly true. Also, the moment you become a TA yourself, you'll realize exactly why you, as an undergrad, were so annoying. _____

Outside Fellowship

If you're ever worried that history will forget the details of your life, holy crap, get a fellowship named after you. These have names like "The Mortimer H. L. Nussenzweig, PhD Class of 1951 Doctoral Fellowship for the Playing of the Zither," and are as difficult to land as they are to fit into one line on your résumé. _____

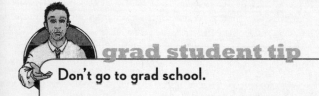

grad student tip

Don't go to grad school.

On-Campus Job

Yeah. Awesome idea. You don't spend enough time on campus as it is. Now you have to spend twenty hours a week working in the library's Special Collections Room or fielding calls from confused tenured professors at the Computer Help Desk. "Well," you think, "at least it pays better than waiting tables." But it doesn't. _____

13

Off-Campus Job

Something probably makes you feel good about being the smartest waitress at Applebee's—briefly, anyway. You can spend all day thinking about the master of fine arts degree you're getting at night while you serve high-school kids who order the cheapest items on the menu. You pity your co-workers who'll still be bussing tables three years from now, but then you realize you'll still be bussing tables three years from now as well—and you'll have a giant debt.   _____

grad student tip

Grad schools like to see that you're an independent thinker. On your grad school application, do not write, "This subject fascinates me because my parents said it does."

Your Parents

During college, your parents were so proud of everything their brilliant little scholar accomplished. But ask them to support you financially during grad school, and watch how fast they backpedal on their commitment to education: "Well...that seventeen-year PhD program sure looks nice, but don't you want to...I don't know, get a job now?"   _____

Student Loan

Thirty years from now, when you look at your hard-earned diploma, you'll reminisce about the good times you spent studying the subject you love. Then you'll sigh, dig out your checkbook, and make another monthly payment. _____

Sallie Mae

This is the name of your great-aunt on your mother's side. She is wealthy. Kill her and take the money. _____

Aunt Sallie Mae

Um . . . You Know . . . Someplace

Most students plan to fund their graduate education by acquiring a large sum of money from um . . . you know . . . someplace. Don't listen to the dissidents who tell you this plan won't work. It must, because you've already made several decisions that require it to have worked. _____

TOTAL: _____

grad student tip

If you own a T-shirt with a picture of Maxwell's equations, the periodic table, or the Muppets, and you don't go to grad school, everyone will wonder why.

2

Selecting a Graduate Program

WHERE, WHEN, HOW, AND WHY, GOD, WHY?

SO YOU'VE decided to go to grad school. That's ... great. Really tremendous. Hooray you.

But which school should you choose? How will you get in? And what's that vague, plaintive wail? Oh, never mind. It's just your soul.

Quiet, soul! Let's take a look at the factors (besides gullibility) that will inform your choice of graduate program.

Agin' Fetish

Unlike high school, where a middle-age student would get (a) funny looks and (b) arrested, graduate schools welcome students of all ages. (They say you're never too old to learn, but that's probably because they've never seen my grandparents try to use the Internet.)

The age at which you opt to begin graduate study says a lot

about you as a person. It invites judgment about the choices you've made—or, rather, about whether you're old enough to know better than to make one particularly unfortunate choice. Here are the messages you project when you enter grad school at different ages:

21–25: You are a serious student who thinks time between college and grad school is time wasted. Though you may have a few lingering traces of party instinct, the real world will soon kill those. (Seven-dollar beers seem a bit less attractive when you're paying your gas bill.)

26–35: You've taken a few years after college to find yourself, work at a well-paying job, or join the Peace Corps, and now it's time to get serious. You always knew you'd come back to grad school, and now here you are, with a little perspective to boot. Hopefully you saved some money.

36–49: At some point in the prime of your life, you realized you wanted a change of career. Doing the math, you discovered you had just enough time left to get this degree, pursue your dreams, and live those dreams for a good decade or so before retirement. Of all age groups, you are the most passionate about learning and don't care whether the younger students think you're a suck-up—which you are. But screw them. This is your time.

≥50: You are unrealistic. You will die before you get to do anything useful with this degree. You are throwing away everything you've worked for. Your family thinks you're off your nut. You really don't understand the way the world works. *You are a ninja.*

The Elegant University

If you could go anywhere you wanted, which grad school would you attend?

Oh. If you could go anywhere you wanted, you wouldn't go to grad school. Very clever. But suppose you've decided to go to grad school. What type of school is right for you?

Small Liberal Arts College

If you like a big piece of tofu on a bed of tempeh and seitan, if you have a pierced tattoo, or if your thick glasses evoke "indie bassist" rather than "1972 NASA Mission Control," you may find a home among the fair-trade coffee shops and lesbian political rallies of a small liberal arts college. (Here, *liberal* refers to most professors' political affiliation, and *small* refers to their ambition.)

Ag School

An institution where classroom size is measured in acres, students chew sorghum, and even the cows have their own mascot ("Hubert the Human"), an ag school makes sense for graduate study only if, say, you want a PhD in dairy science. But if you want a PhD in dairy science...why? Are you trying to be King of the Farmers?

grad student tip

The GRE is a "computer-adaptive" test, which means that the questions get harder if you answer previous questions correctly. It also means that if an easy question comes up, you'll totally freak out and worry that you missed the last question.

Freeze-Your-Ass-Off College

Isn't upstate New York beautiful in the spring? And Wisconsin. Isn't Wisconsin beautiful in the spring? Yeah. That's why they show you these schools *in the spring*. Remember, if a school has a charming series of tunnels connecting its academic buildings, it's because the great outdoors is absolutely glacial eight months a year.

Ivy League University

Do you enjoy dining on white linen tablecloths, ordering servants to polish the silver, and having your every whim catered to? That's not important. The real question is, do you enjoy *watching undergrads* dine on white linen tablecloths, order servants to polish the silver, and have their every whim catered to? Your sole function at these schools is to provide the undergrads with something to bitch about. ("I can't understand my TA's accent because he's from the middle class!") Should you enroll at an Ivy League grad school, look forward to interacting with highly intelligent, highly whiny students, all of whom have trust funds set up to pay the legal fees incurred when they sue your ass for giving them a B+.

School Outside the United States

It's bold to commit oneself to several years in a strange country with a strange language and customs, such as Finland or Texas. But graduate study abroad is perfect for the show-off student who feels that since Applied Mathematics isn't difficult enough—hell, let's do it in Mandarin. Should you

grad student tip

Due to recent changes by the Educational Testing Service, the GRE will no longer include a penmanship test, Sudoku, or the swimsuit competition.

choose to go international, you'll quickly find yourself the lone token defender of America's foreign policy—even if you hate America's foreign policy—not to mention the only student bored by constant discussion of soccer. On the upside, every other nation has better beer.

Party School

Be forewarned that the word *party* does not apply to you. *Party* is the term for the horrible, drunken brawl in the next apartment that interrupts you during a late-night study session. *Party* is the excuse your students will give you for missing class. *Party* is a culture you may have once loved but will quickly grow to despise. Over the course of your graduate studies, *party* will age you fifty years. You'll scarcely notice that you've suddenly become an elderly crank, banging on your apartment wall, berating "those damn fool kids," wishing that one of them, *just one*, might hook up with you.

Low-Cost-of-Living School

There is one way to survive grad school without impoverishing yourself, but it's not pretty: Find a college whose two-story academic buildings are the tallest structures in town. Make sure it's surrounded by wheat fields, industrial waste, and/or bands of migrant timberwolves. And a Wal-Mart. Then pat yourself on the back as you smugly pay your twenty-dollar monthly rent, because *wow*. You're saving so *much money*. (Yeah. You're saving it for plane tickets to get as far the hell away as often as possible.)

Distance Learning Academy

Want an advanced degree without the drudgery of human interaction, scholarly discussion, or personal enrichment? Now you can "attend" grad school by simply posting grammatically unfortunate comments on message boards! Distance learning—so called because it allows you to "distance" yourself from "learning"—lets you attend class while checking your email, updating your Facebook status, or surfing for YouTube videos of funny kittens. Now *that's* a degree to be proud of.

Safety School

A safety school is a school you *know* you'll get into, you convince yourself you'd gladly attend, and then, when it's the only school that admits you, one about which you bitch and moan because you really aren't content there. While there, you'll feel compelled to ensure that all the other grad students know it's your safety school. This will make them love you.

grad student tip

Translate a school's motto into English before choosing that school. Avoid, for example, schools whose mottos are "Lasciate Ogne Speranza, Voi Ch'entrate" or "Arbeit Macht Frei."

In Quad We Trust

Once you decide which grad school to attend, visit the campus. Maybe even take a campus tour so that you can hear the undergraduate tour guides tell the same apocryphal stories you hear at every school ("The library is sinking because when the architect designed it, *he forgot to take into account the weight of the books!*").

Check out pages 26–27, then take a look around your campus. Learn the names of the buildings. Harass a squirrel or two.

And get comfortable, bitch, because you're gonna be here a *long* time.

Not Overly Invested

Smart financial planners recommend sound investment strategies, consultation with professionals, and lucrative interest-bearing accounts. Then again, smart financial planners have lots of money. You, not so much.

But with the few assets you have, it's still a good idea to diversify. Let's take a look at a grad student's well-balanced portfolio:

Checking Account	$10.71
Savings Account	$40.00
Inadvertent Savings Account (between couch cushions)	$1.27
Collateral (value of couch)	$1.08
Partially Full Photocopy Card	$2.10
Unused Postage Stamp	$0.44
Unrealized Beer Bottle Deposits	$0.15
Anticipated Birthday Gift (just ten months to go!)	$25.00

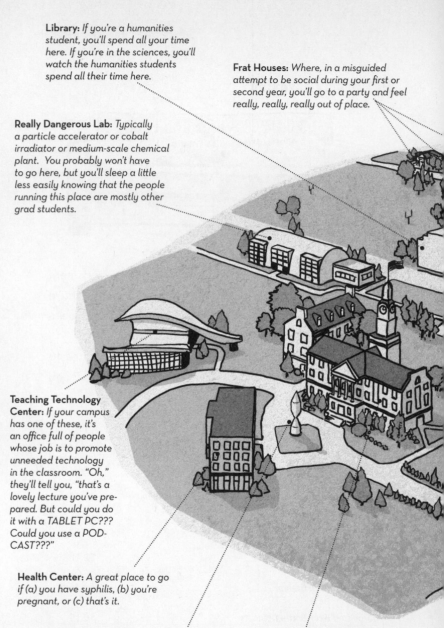

Library: *If you're a humanities student, you'll spend all your time here. If you're in the sciences, you'll watch the humanities students spend all their time here.*

Frat Houses: *Where, in a misguided attempt to be social during your first or second year, you'll go to a party and feel really, really, really out of place.*

Really Dangerous Lab: *Typically a particle accelerator or cobalt irradiator or medium-scale chemical plant. You probably won't have to go here, but you'll sleep a little less easily knowing that the people running this place are mostly other grad students.*

Teaching Technology Center: *If your campus has one of these, it's an office full of people whose job is to promote unneeded technology in the classroom. "Oh," they'll tell you, "that's a lovely lecture you've prepared. But could you do it with a TABLET PC??? Could you use a POD-CAST???"*

Health Center: *A great place to go if (a) you have syphilis, (b) you're pregnant, or (c) that's it.*

Stupid Traditional Object: *A big rock that everyone paints, or a gate you're not allowed to walk through, or a statue whose foot people rub for luck, or some other ridiculous crap. Undergrads are dumb.*

Career Services: *Home of ambiguous pamphlets, a public computer that can access only the Career Services website, and helpful résumé counselors who can give you a range of font- and layout-based advice.*

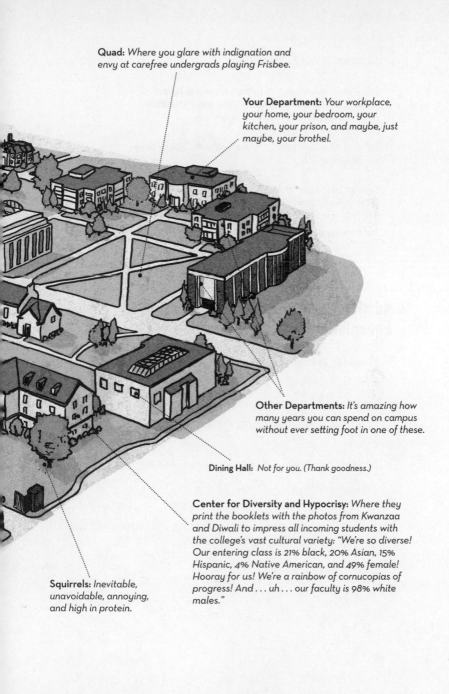

Quad: *Where you glare with indignation and envy at carefree undergrads playing Frisbee.*

Your Department: *Your workplace, your home, your bedroom, your kitchen, your prison, and maybe, just maybe, your brothel.*

Other Departments: *It's amazing how many years you can spend on campus without ever setting foot in one of these.*

Dining Hall: *Not for you. (Thank goodness.)*

Center for Diversity and Hypocrisy: *Where they print the booklets with the photos from Kwanzaa and Diwali to impress all incoming students with the college's vast cultural variety: "We're so diverse! Our entering class is 21% black, 20% Asian, 15% Hispanic, 4% Native American, and 49% female! Hooray for us! We're a rainbow of cornucopias of progress! And . . . uh . . . our faculty is 98% white males."*

Squirrels: *Inevitable, unavoidable, annoying, and high in protein.*

Significant Mutual Fund Holdings	Just kidding
Lost Cash Probably Buried Under Proust and Narrative Allegory, Vol. 6, *in Library Carrel (and when you find it, you'll use it to top off the photocopy card)*	$5.00
Value of Wine Collection (i.e., the bottle of Charles Shaw you bought at Trader Joe's)	$2.99
Current Total Value of All Nearby Take-a-Penny-Leave-a-Penny Trays	$0.73
Outstanding Debt	AAAAAAAH! DON'T LOOK! DON'T LOOK!

Admission Accomplished: Selecting the Least Egregious Recommendation Letter

Because grades, GRE scores, and application essays are all poor predictors of academic ability, grad school admissions committees demand something a bit more reliable: a hastily written recommendation from someone you handpicked to praise you.

Most schools will want to see an unreasonable number of these, such as three. Which do you choose? Whose say-so is sufficient to convince the committee? (And why in God's name did you wait until two days before the letters were due?)

Let's move down the hierarchy:

Professor Who Knows You Well and Likes You

This is the holy grail of recommendation letters. You may even know such a professor—but do you know *three*? Probably not.

Professor Who Knows You Well but Doesn't Like You

Risky. Some professors who don't like you can be diplomatic and at least make vague or neutral statements such as "He certainly gets things done," or "She is a student." But others will refuse to write a reference letter, or, worse, will write only negative sentiments. If this happens, call your admissions committee and tell them you accidentally told this professor it was Opposite Day.

Professor Who Doesn't Know You

In a lecture course of five hundred students, you ended up somewhere in the upper third. You are automatically entitled to ask the professor for a recommendation letter, which will probably look something like this:

I've known this student for five minutes, and she's the best student I met during those five minutes. She scored above average in my class. She gave me a copy of her résumé to help me write this letter. It looks okay. I'm attaching it.

Really Famous and Distinguished Person Who Doesn't Know You

So your dad once shared an elevator with the prime minister of Singapore, and he wants the guy to write you a recommendation. Unfortunately, admissions committees aren't as dumb as you'd think, and they can tell when you're celebrity-baiting—not that this realization will necessarily stop them from admitting you.

Teaching Assistant

Grad students recommending grad students? Preposterous! You really think your twenty-four-year-old TA from Intro to Psychology has an ounce of clout with an admissions committee? "But I *know* my TA," you're probably saying, "and I've never talked to my professor." That's like a restaurant critic saying, "I've never tasted the food, but I've developed quite a relationship with the napkin." Sounds to me like someone squandered valuable office hours, which are meant to be meet-your-professor schmooze-a-thons.

Non-Academic Employer

If you have letters from one science professor and one humanities professor, consider balancing these with a note from your shift supervisor at Red Lobster. Sure, such a letter may not attest to your academic abilities. And you're practically telling the admissions committee that your most relevant skill is your ability to make large margaritas. But if the letter smells like those warm cheesy biscuits, you're in.

Clergyperson

If, rather than reading good books, you spent your college career reading the Good Book, you might ask your clergyperson for a reference letter. You might also end up with a letter full of comments unlikely to help your cause, such as "He was the cutest altar boy *ever*" or "I spent her formative years convincing her that evolution is a myth. Undo *that*, Professor Smarty Pants."

Athletic Coach

Beware! This tactic may have worked very well to get you into college, but it won't work for grad school. For college, these recommendations usually contain a total of two sentences, typically something like, "She captained the all-state rowing team. You want that." And colleges actually climb all over one another to admit the student. "I don't care if he's functionally illiterate!" the university president screams, "he can throw a ball through a hoop!" Grad schools, however, have no such equivalent; no one has ever been admitted so that their department's softball team can totally trounce the Mechanical Engineering department's softball team.

Parent

Seriously? This is the best you can come up with? "If Mom says I have a good work ethic, it *must* be true!" Your only hope of having a parent's letter get you into grad school is if your parent (a) teaches at a university, (b) has a different last name from yours, and (c) can refrain from calling you "my wittle dumpling."

"Available Upon Request"

Writing this magical phrase tells the admissions committee that, in order to hear from your references, they'll need to ask you specifically. It also neglects the fact that the application *does* ask you specifically. But if you plan ultimately never to submit any reference letters...yeah, you could go this route.

"Available Upon Bequest"

Writing this magical phrase tells the admissions committee that they can have their recommendation letters when they pry them from your cold, dead hands.

Caste of Thousands

Chickens may seem haphazard. But watch them eat, and you'll notice that their society obeys a rigidly stratified "pecking order," with the most important chickens eating first. Typically, these are the chickens who have tenure.

Your school has a pecking order, too, one that dates back to feudalism. While some elements of the university system have evolved since the Middle Ages (thirteenth-century Byzantine scholars probably didn't have wireless Internet, for example—though try explaining that to a group of undergrads), some medieval practices remain intact, in particular the idea that the many serve the few.

Guess which group you're in! Here's a hint: Your school has *many* grad students.

This diagram illustrates your level of importance within the university hierarchy. (And just so you know, though they don't appear in the pyramid, you do rank below tenured chickens.)

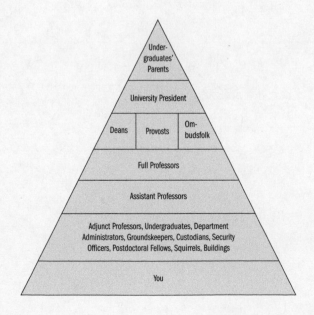

3

Grad Student Life

YOU WEREN'T GOING TO DO MUCH WITH YOUR

TWENTIES ANYWAY

MERRIAM-WEBSTER defines *life* as "an organismic state characterized by capacity for metabolism, growth, reaction to stimuli, and reproduction."

In this sense, grad students technically display the qualities of life, in that they

a. **metabolize** as much free food as they can steal,

b. **grow** beards or leg hair from inattention to hygiene,

c. **react** to the amount of work they have to do tonight with incredulity and screams of pure terror, and

d. **reproduce** anything their advisors ask them to photocopy.

Contrarily, the *Oxford English Dictionary* defines *life* as "something grad students do not have."

What constitutes grad student life? How do advanced degree candidates spend their non-working hours? And, most important, which pieces don't fit in the other chapters of this book? Let's find out.

Old School: A Brief History of Grad Students

Philosopher George Santayana once said that those who do not recall their history are doomed to repeat it. Or maybe Winston Churchill said that. I don't know. I can't recall my history.

Grad students have roamed the earth for millennia, evolving from single-cell forms (paramecia were known as "the grad students of eukaryotic protozoa") to the stooped, hairy, grunting creatures of the Pleistocene epoch (*Homo academicus*), to the stooped, hairy, grunting creatures of today.

Let's take a look at our shared past. In this section, we'll activate the Wayback Machine, fire up that flux capacitor, and, uh, do whatever Urkel did when he traveled back in time. Annoy Carl Winslow, I think. And all of us, too.

And remember: Those who do not recall their history are doomed to repeat it. Did I already write that? I can't recall.

c. 2000 BC Thog of Gronk, the world's first graduate student, begins his PhD program. His department's stipend, four pointy rocks, has not increased to this day.

0 The birth of Jesus of Nazareth is attended by his thesis committee of three tenured wise men bearing gifts of frankincense, myrrh, and a stack of papers to grade.

AD 18 Jesus amazes grad students everywhere by turning water into a medium-quality, well-priced microbrew.

1849 While traveling the Oregon Trail on his way to study at Willamette Valley University, a grad student contracts dysentery and dies, despite his ability to fell a bison with a single square bullet. He is buried in a shallow grave with a small, humorous headstone.

1923 Physicist Werner Heisenberg receives his doctorate in Munich, later discovering the Uncertainty Principle, which states that the more likely one is to understand the Uncertainty Principle, the less likely one is to get a date.

1933 Adolf Hitler establishes work camps in which residents are forced to labor relentlessly with little reward under the false pretense that hard work will bring freedom. Jewish grad students fail to notice the change.

1950 While earning a PhD in economics, grad student John "Russell Crowe" Nash formulates Non-Cooperative Game Theory. Friends and family question Nash's sanity when he experiences visual delusions, harbors paranoid fantasies, and appears to enjoy grad school.

1968 Counterculture message of the turbulent 1960s hits grad students, who pledge to fight the power by turning on, tuning in, and dropping out of their graduate programs after only a decade. Before this can happen, though, the 1970s arrive, and everyone grows creepy moustaches, making them particularly suited to remain in academia.

1973 While in grad school, Frank Wilczek discovers the concept of asymptotic freedom, eventually earning a Nobel Prize in physics. What have *you* done?

1983 Prince Adam of Eternia, attending Castle Grayskull University (Go Battle Cats!), earns his MU degree (Master's of the Universe).

2008 In a demonstration of the disparity between workloads in postgraduate programs, Neil Patrick Harris, having become an MD at age fourteen, completes a nineteen-year PhD in Horribleness.

2008 Economic meltdown affects millions, instantly halving the value of 401(k) plans and plunging the stock market to record lows. Grad students are unaffected because *a fraction of zero is still zero*.

2010 In a victory for nerds everywhere, a publisher actually thinks a book with a Heisenberg joke is marketable.

2020 Good evening. I'm Hugh Downs. And I'm Barbara Walters.

2038 You graduate.

802,701 H. G. Wells arrives in the distant future and discovers the Morlocks, a race doomed to toil fruitlessly in misery and subterranean darkness. (Insert easy joke about grad students here.)

grad student tip

Shut up about where you went to college. No one wants to hear it.

Tool Sample

The Indian philosopher Baloo once spoke of the "simple bare necessities of life," which apparently included food, water, shelter, and a half-clothed feral boy.

As a grad student, your needs are a bit different—not so many feral boys, for example (unless you're studying psychology, in which case you'll need several). Everything you require to survive grad school can be found in one handy toolbox. It's much like Batman's utility belt, except it's not a belt, and you, my friend, are no Batman.

The following items are found in your Grad Student Toolbox:

Coffee Mug

A coffee mug is the conduit by which you convey caffeine into your blood, largely because society frowns upon drinking directly from coffeepots or injecting espresso into one's cephalic vein. When selecting a mug, choose one that can withstand abuse. Ceramic mugs may look nice, but only a shatterproof plastic or acrylic mug will still hold coffee by the time you graduate. (To test your mug, slam it on the ground repeatedly and yell, "I can't take it anymore!")

Eyeglasses

Tacitly implying that your vision has deteriorated from long nights of studying in dimly lit spaces, eyeglasses are the first sign that you've willingly sacrificed health in favor of knowledge. "The ability to see is fleeting," lenses seem to broadcast, "but love of Chaucer is forever." (This message assumes your topic of study is Chaucer, which is only true for about half of all grad students.) Of course, not all grad students have impaired vision, but even so, you know deep down that your soul is the soul of a person who wears eyeglasses. Unfashionable ones, too.

Watch

In graduate school, it's important to keep accurate time so that you have something to disregard. When you're in the library or lab and you tell someone, "I should be done in about half an hour," you really mean that in two hours you'll tell them you'll be done in fifteen minutes. In a way, this action is a microcosm of grad school itself: "Seriously. I'll graduate in three months. And this year I mean it."

Hat

For those days when basic hygiene doesn't fit with your schedule, adding a hat to your repertoire can do a world of good. A hat calms untamed hair, casts a welcome shadow on a greasy face, and, with its handy brim, keeps people just a few inches farther away from unbrushed teeth. Call it your "I-have-not-yet-taken-a-shower cap." Also, if you smell bad, your colleagues will just think you're wearing a smelly hat.

Grappling Hook

Granted, you probably won't need this in grad school. But HOW FRICKIN' COOL WOULD IT BE IF YOU DID???

Cheat Sheet

Most grad students have the integrity not to cheat on exams. They do, however, need "cheat sheets" to tell them how to interact with other humans who aren't in their department, a skill they often forget. Here's a sample:

> Start with a greeting, such as "Hi," "Hello," or "Hey."
> **DO NOT MENTION YOUR RESEARCH!**
>
> Inquire after your conversation partner's health or general status. Try "How's it going?" or "How've you been?"
> **DO NOT MENTION YOUR RESEARCH!**

Even with a cheat sheet, grad students sometimes mess this up:

NORMAL PERSON: Hi.

GRAD STUDENT: Hello! Let k be any integer such that . . .

Paper

Remember the kind of paper you wrote on in kindergarten? The distance between the horizontal lines was wider than your arm, and there was even room for that middle dotted line. Then you graduated to regular paper and, eventually, in a transition that assured you unquestionably of your reaching adulthood, to *college ruled* paper. Unfortunately, there is no "grad school ruled" paper, but different disciplines do find different types of paper indispensable:

Engineering: graph paper

Environmental science: recycled paper

Architecture: very big paper

History: parchment

Law school: Uh, I don't know. Legal pads?

Computer science: What's paper?

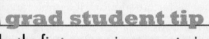

grad student tip

Don't be the first person in your entering class to get drunk. Just don't.

On the other hand, some items are very specifically *not* in the Grad Student Toolbox:

Pens

There are no pens in your toolbox—not because you don't need them, but because you don't need to actively obtain them. In a world where every commodity is carefully tracked and distributed, pens are the exception, floating freely in unoccupied space. You may have a pen with you right now, but if you don't, you could certainly find one in a couple of minutes, and no one would mind if you took it. No other product is like this: You don't drive your car, drop it off somewhere, and grab the next one you see lying around. Pens are rarely used start to finish by the same person. When was the last time you bought a pen, used it for a long time, and saw it through to the end of its ink supply? Or bought an actual replacement ball-point cartridge? Never. Look at the pen nearest you right now. Do you even know where it came from? Is it imprinted with the logo of a company you've never heard of? We spend our lives drifting through an ephemeral sea of pens, using them and letting them go, like spent lovers—finding, lending, misplacing, replacing, discovering, dismantling, piling the components on our desks and playing with that little spring. If there is any evidence for creationism, it can be found in pens: They exist all around us, but no one knows from whence they came. We know only that they are good, they are here to serve us, and some people can spin them around their thumb.

Book to Read for Pleasure

You tell yourself you'll have time to read for pleasure in grad school, but honestly, you won't. (Unless it's this book. You have time for this book. It's literary gold.)

grad student tip

Scratch this box and sniff the paper. Smell that? Smells like paper. Get used to it.

Wallet

Why carry something that's empty?

grad student tip

Beware of seminars whose titles are structured as "Something Interesting: Something Boring." For example: "Sex, Drugs, and Rock and Roll: Hydroxymethylcarbonyl Isotere-Based Dipeptidomimetics Targeting Malarial Aspartic Protease Plasmepsin."

Grad's Anatomy

Whoa. This next page is like looking in a mirror, isn't it? Yep. Just like looking in a medium-resolution gray-scale mirror with captions that makes everything the size of a trade paperback.

Sorry to blow your mind, but this is no mirror. It's a diagram showing the most important parts of the average grad student. Use it to identify grad students from afar or, at the very least, to engage in a very specific game of Hokey Pokey.

grad student tip

You have a lot to do during your first week on campus, such as registering for classes, meeting your advisor, and seeing if the health center stocks Zoloft.

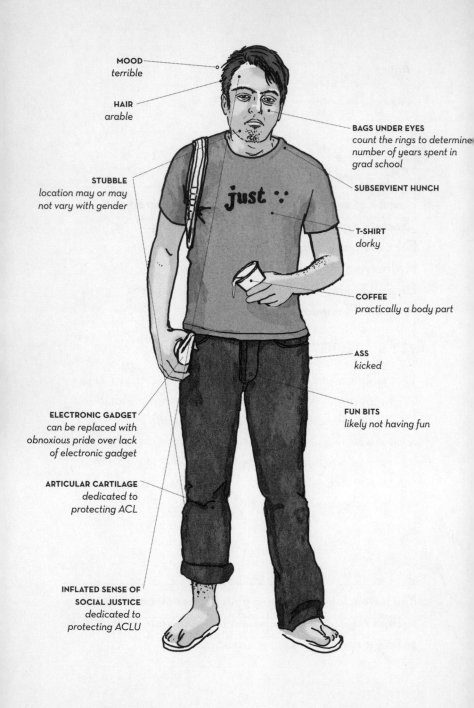

MOOD
terrible

HAIR
arable

BAGS UNDER EYES
count the rings to determine number of years spent in grad school

STUBBLE
location may or may not vary with gender

SUBSERVIENT HUNCH

T-SHIRT
dorky

COFFEE
practically a body part

ASS
kicked

ELECTRONIC GADGET
can be replaced with obnoxious pride over lack of electronic gadget

FUN BITS
likely not having fun

ARTICULAR CARTILAGE
dedicated to protecting ACL

INFLATED SENSE OF SOCIAL JUSTICE
dedicated to protecting ACLU

Resenting Presenting

The 2006 International Welfare Act banned torture by sleep deprivation. Unfortunately, the provision did not extend to the departmental seminar, where dozens of students are forced to watch a tedious presentation in uncomfortable chairs, heads lolling back like the tops of Pez dispensers.

Let's be honest. When speakers present their research, you *try* to pay attention. You *try* to follow their best attempts at obfuscation. But after about five minutes, the pretty pictures on the inside of your eyelids become quite attractive.

Every seminar is different, in the same way that the circles of Hell are different. But they share some of the same unfortunate qualities, too. After you've stolen the requisite bagel, watch for the following to happen in your next departmental seminar:

- The speaker will read a wordy slide verbatim, thus defeating the purpose of a talk.

- Something won't transfer from Mac to PC.

- The faculty member who once glared at you for falling asleep will fall asleep.

- A poor, misguided student will actually take notes.

- The projector will malfunction, and a room full of PhD's will be unable to fix it.

- The speaker will explain abbreviations and acronyms more quickly than can be realistically remembered, leading no one in the room to marvel when he concludes, "And it turned out the answer was a combination of DMSO and PLM4!"

- A slide will include unnecessary animation, and results will spiral or bounce into place while the speaker grins and everyone under thirty rolls their eyes.

- You will become painfully aware that it's a beautiful day outside.

- You will doodle. It will be pretty.

- You will start writing a list of things you need to accomplish as soon as they let you out of this freaking room.

- The speaker will spend ten minutes thanking people no one in the room has heard of.

- If the speaker has a laser pointer, he will laser-point to items to which lasers needn't point.

- The speaker will make statements clearly designed to demonstrate that he is smarter than you. He will alternate this practice with long, laborious explanations of something all attendees know already.

- Spittle will be visible.

- The student who asks every speaker a question . . . will ask the speaker a question.

- The slideshow will advance too far by accident, and the speaker will need help finding the "back" button.

- If the speaker uses actual transparencies or gives an old-school "chalk talk," he will act all superior about it.

- The final slide will include a cute cartoon. Too little, too late.

- Fifteen minutes past the scheduled end time, there will be no end in sight. *Is nothing sacred?*

YourSpace

Remember that grad students are technically employees of the university (unless it's a matter of health insurance, benefits, parking, unionization, or living wage). A natural question on your first day is "Where might I find my office?" And a natural answer is, of course, "Ha ha ha ha ha! Your office? You think you're getting an office? Are you the Queen Mother? Your *office*?"

Sorry, Your Majesty. Only a few rare grad students ever get their own office, and this fact only gets them beaten up anyway. What space do you have, then, to call your own?

Library Carrel

A library carrel, the place to stash all your obscure books no one else wants to use anyway, is what results when someone starts building a cubicle and gives up. Your carrel is your school's reluctant acknowledgment that you'd kill someone if you had to share library tables with undergrads demanding to know why they can't use Facebook on the library catalog computer.

Lab Bench

If you're one of those science types, you may get your own little plot of laboratory real estate, where you store your bottles of toxic whatnot in exactly the sort of disarray only you can understand. And God help the student at the next bench who steals your Sharpie.

Outdoors

When you're young and naïve, you picture yourself idyllically toting some work outside, lying on a verdant quad, sipping iced tea, and loving life. But you learn a lot about yourself the first time you try to work outside. Specifically, you learn that you don't want to work outside. The ground isn't actually soft—at least not compared to, say, a chair. Your laptop screen does not glow nearly as brightly as you thought it would. And all around you, undergrads yell inanities as they copulate on the quad.

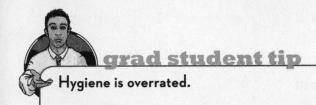

grad student tip

Hygiene is overrated.

Lap

Your lap is Nature's desk—or at least that's your school's rationale for not giving you a real desk. Perfect for holding books and highly portable, your lap is the intended substrate for your laptop—and the best part is, no matter what, no one can ever take your lap away from you (unless they tell you to stand up).

Coffee Shop

You feel sophisticated when you work at a coffee shop, like an urbane urbanite, a polite cosmopolite, huddled in a corner (where the AC power outlet is) and sipping the largest, most espresso-filled drink they offer. You are not meant to be caged in a small office, you tell yourself—you are a person of the people. Not that you were ever offered a small office, but that's not the point.

Home

Home is not a place for doing work; it is a place for relaxing. For the sake of your mental health, keep the two aspects of your life separate, and make sure never to bring your work home.

Just kidding. In grad school, you'll do so *much fucking work* at home.

Public Transit

Read an advanced textbook with an unpronounceable title on the bus, and you'll earn the respect of everyone listening to iPods or pretending not to stare at other passengers. "Who is that mysterious genius?" they'll wonder. "Why didn't that mysterious genius shower?"

Shared Crappy Office

This is the holy grail of spaces to occupy—which is sad. You get four walls, a door, and a desk, and a whole group of colleagues who talk loudly on the phone and repeatedly demand that you look at distracting websites.

Inconspicuous Consumption

Grad school is filled with special events designed to enrich your intellectual experience. But who gives a shit?

More important, many of these events offer free food—but you have to schedule your mooching carefully. You're a busy person. You can't waste time sitting through a boring talk only to learn that the bagels you saw on your way in are meant for something else.

Stealing food is not wrong. Foxes steal food. In fact, foxes steal live chickens. Are foxes immoral? No. Foxes are cute. So follow the example of the noble fox and use this handy guide to your new snack-filled universe. (And if, for some strange reason, your grad school affords you the opportunity to steal live chickens—do it.)

EVENT: Seminar/Colloquium

Likelihood of Free Food: Varies

Pros: If the seminar is run by someone unfamiliar with the mysterious ways of grad students, they may be stupid enough to set the food out before the talk begins. Then you can wander by, steal food, and—oh no!—suddenly remember something else you have to do. Let's go, Free Doughnut. We've got places to be.

Cons: If the food is served *after* the seminar, you may have to pretend you sat through it. You'll wander among the post-seminar crowd saying things like "I think the most exciting part of this talk was the middle," convincing the masses that you shared their ordeal. Watch out for the overzealous Free Food Protector, who might slap your hand away from the food and say, "Aha! I know you're lying—the seminar *had no middle!*"

EVENT: Mandatory Safety Training

Likelihood of Free Food: Low

Pros: You'll learn how the fire extinguishers work, or where the chemical showers are, or how much radiation they've arranged for you to regularly ingest. Could be useful.

Cons: There's rarely free food, and the "useful" part of the training will occupy two or three minutes. The rest will consist of the warning

"Be safe" repeated over and over again. There might even be a mandatory quiz that was clearly written for brilliant people:

1. You come across unexploded munitions and decide to whack them with a hammer. Is this safe or unsafe?

2. Draw a funny animal mascot promoting safety.

EVENT: Holiday Party

Likelihood of Free Food: High

Pros: In the spirit of the holiday season, no one can deny you a little free food. You're like Tiny Tim—the child, not the entertainer.

Cons: This is one of the few times your department may serve you alcohol, which is great—until you realize that *all of the professors are getting drunk, too.* It only takes one butt slap from a ninety-year-old cultural anthropologist to make you want to give up both drinking and Christmas.

EVENT: Distinguished Professor So-and-So from Elsewhere Tours the Department

Likelihood of Free Food: High

Pros: Departments like to deceive visiting dignitaries. They'll casually fill all empty spaces with food—and good food, too. Food that needs to sit in a steam tray. Food heated with cans of Sterno. Crab dip. Chicken satay skewers. Little pita triangles. *Real-people food.*

Cons: This food is based on a lie. Your department wants the dignitary to think you celebrate this way all the time, that trays of crudités and assorted cheese cubes sit out in your department lobby every day.

More Pros: Free food based on a lie is still free food.

EVENT: Department Halloween Party

Likelihood of Free Food: High

Pros: If you don't already have something you call your "Candy Drawer," now's the time to establish one. Candy transports well and keeps for months, so be sure to wear a shapeless costume with lots of internal pockets—i.e., dress as a ghost, a priest, or a candy thief.

Cons: You have to put up with all the dorky bullshit that academics trot out on Halloween. Someone always dresses as a student of a different discipline and thinks it's hilarious. ("I'm a molecular biochemist, but I'm dressed as a molecular biophysicist! Ha ha ha ha ha!")

EVENT: Exam Grading

Likelihood of Free Food: Medium to High

Pros: When professors ask you to do their job for them, they know you need a little extra encouragement. Grading a stack of three hundred exams is such a heinous job that free pizza may not make up for it, but it will somewhat ease the pain of reading another illiterate lacrosse player's attempt to fudge his way through the essay questions.

Cons: The pizza will keep you happy for an hour. Exam grading may last six hours. Sucker!

EVENT: Foody McFreeFood's Free Food Bonanza, with Free Food

Likelihood of Free Food: Very High

Pros: This event features tons and tons of free food.

Cons: This event does not exist.

A special note on bagels: Free bagels are great. You can legitimately call them breakfast, lunch, or a snack. You can even call them dinner if you're a hobo, which you might be. You stare at the tray of yeasty tori outside a seminar, marveling at the wonderful variety of flavors. Cinnamon raisin! Chocolate chip! Pumpernickel! Truly, we live in the best of all possible worlds.

But beware, for the bagels hold a deep, dark secret: the onion bagel.

The function of an onion bagel is to make all other bagels in a half-mile radius smell and taste like the onion bagel. Just as you're enjoying a mouthful of, say, sweet cranberry goodness—you stop. Sniff. Lick tentatively. Could it be? *Curse you, Onion Bagel!*

If only, by some miracle, you could intervene at the moment of purchase. "Let's see," your department administrator probably said while waiting at the supermarket bakery. "We'll get a dozen plain bagels. A dozen sesame seed. Half a dozen blue-berry. And what are those? Gingerbread bagels? Ooh, how seasonal. A half dozen of those, please ..."

Stopstopstop oh please stop, just pay for the bagels and go, oh pleasepleaseplease—

"...and one onion bagel. Just to fuck with the grad students."

Noooooooooooooooooo!

Recipes for Success

Grad students cannot live on free bagels alone. Free bagels fulfill only one of the four food groups (the "Freebie" group), the other three being the "Outright Stolen" group, the "Temporarily Hidden Until Its Rightful Owner Forgets About It" group, and of course, the (use sparingly!) "Food Purchased and Cooked Yourself" group.

When you absolutely must prepare your own food, try one of these special grad student recipes. Bon appétit! (That's French for "Get back to work!")

Fast-acting Coffee

INGREDIENTS / EQUIPMENT

Coffee beans   Plastic stirring straw
Bean grinder

INSTRUCTIONS

1. Grind the coffee beans to a very fine powder.
2. With one end of the coffee straw in your nostril, snort the powder.
3. Wheeeeeeeeeeeeeeeee!

Roasted Undergrad on a Spit

INGREDIENTS / EQUIPMENT

Barbecue pit
Open flame
Your favorite undergrad

INSTRUCTIONS

1. Skewer the undergrad on a spit, taking care to run the iron rod from the student's pampered ass through his or her lying mouth.

2. As you rotate the spit over the open flame, instruct the undergrad to tell you again why he or she deserves to have the last exam regraded.

3. Wake up and sigh wistfully. *Someday.*

Thesis Committee Bribery Brownies

INGREDIENTS / EQUIPMENT

1 package brownie mix   Copy of paper written by a thesis
Baking pan   committee member

INSTRUCTIONS

1. Prepare brownies as per package directions.

2. Remove all brownies from pan. Line pan with committee member's paper and replace brownies on top.

3. Bring brownies to thesis committee meeting. Tell everyone you've brought brownies for them—and *what's this?* A paper written by a thesis committee member! Guess what must have happened: You were reading the paper for the tenth time because it's *so brilliant,* and it must have fallen into the brownie pan, and you were too busy pondering the paper's wisdom to notice!

Macaroni and Tears

INGREDIENTS/EQUIPMENT

1 pkg. macaroni   The ability to view your life objectively

Bowl

INSTRUCTIONS

1. Cook macaroni and drain into bowl.

2. Think about your life, your progress, and the likelihood that you'll graduate. Think about the years you'll never get back. Think about how much work you have to do tonight.

3. For a rich, salty flavor, be sure to keep the bowl of macaroni right below your face as you think.

Home Cooking

INGREDIENTS/EQUIPMENT

Car or plane

INSTRUCTIONS

1. Get in car or plane.

2. Go home.

3. Eat what your parents cook.

Data Fudge

INGREDIENTS/ EQUIPMENT

12 oz. chocolate   Double boiler

1 pt. heavy cream   Pan

INSTRUCTIONS

1. Measure out 12 oz. of chocolate, but you can say it's 20.

2. Melt chocolate in double boiler for 9 minutes, but make believe it was 15 minutes, pretending to stir constantly.

3. Whisk in the heavy cream, writing down the time at which you added it, give or take an hour.

4. Scoop mixture into pan and tell everyone you allowed it to cool.

Free Food: Is It Possible to Take Too Much?

No.

4

Research and Destroy

MAKING DATA PRETTY

IN THEORY, you're in graduate school to work. (In reality, you're in graduate school to complain about work.)

You've selected a topic that enraptures you so much that you can't imagine doing anything else, primarily because you don't have the time to imagine doing anything else. Unlike college, at grad school you can't change your major, and unlike at an actual job, you can't charge overtime. Your reward for years of drudgery is, if you're lucky, the opportunity to publish your ideas in a small, unpopular journal.

What the hell were you thinking?

Oh. You were thinking that you'd use your intellect to illuminate a tiny corner of the world. How naïve.

Unfortunately, you may not yet understand exactly how tiny that corner is. As you progressed through school, the topic of each class narrowed a bit, and now you're stuck studying only the most focused subjects:

Elementary School	Science
High School	Biology
College, underclassman	Introduction to Animal Behavior
College, upperclassman	Birds of the Americas
Graduate School	Female-Specific Mating Practices of DulBecco's Finch in 138 Square Feet of Peruvian Tundra on Alternate Thursdays and Their Impact on Municipal Waste Collection Policy

Your area of study may be esoteric, your findings may be inconsequential, and you may spend more effort validating your data-gathering method than actually employing it—but, *man,* you are totally gonna rock those 138 square feet of Peruvian tundra.

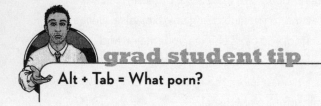

grad student tip

Alt + Tab = What porn?

Your Advisor: Mentor or *Tor*mentor?

Aristotle had Plato. Luke Skywalker had Obi-Wan Kenobi. And you've got some weirdo with big glasses and a nice computer who still thinks your name is Jeff.

Choosing your advisor is one of the most important parts of grad school, as it determines specifically who will take credit

for the work you do. So when it comes time to select someone to oversee you—or overlook you—watch for the following
types of advisor in your department:

The Jet-Setter

This professor's career is
zooming along, and she's on a
tight schedule, giving the keynote address at a different conference every week. For her
graduate students, this means
she won't be able to do a lot of
"hand-holding," or "clarifying," or "mentoring," or "anything."

If she asks how your research is progressing, it's not because she's interested; it's because she's just realized you're
still here.

The Deaf Optimist

Bad news about your research?
Say no more. No, really—say no
more, because she won't hear it.
A typical conversation with the
Deaf Optimist goes something
like this:

You: I've been working on this project for about a year now,
and I don't think it's going anywhere.

OPTIMIST: That's great!

YOU: No, really—I'm positive it's doomed to fail. Maybe I should switch to something else.

OPTIMIST: So you'll have it ready to publish next week?

YOU: You don't understand. I've proven conclusively that this project is a dead end. It's a waste of time, money, and resources. A year of my adult life has been sacrificed in pursuit of the unattainable. Even if you had a hundred grad students working around the clock, they wouldn't make an inch of progress toward this ridiculous goal.

OPTIMIST: Yes, now that you mention it, rainbows *are* beautiful!

There are methods of dealing with the Deaf Optimist, but they all involve weaponry.

grad student tip

Your campus library designates certain books as "noncirculating." This is the library's way of practically begging you to steal them.

The Tenure Master

This professor received tenure in 1970 and—coincidentally!—has not published anything since 1970. The very day his name alone was deemed sufficient to glean a university salary for life, he stopped his research, boarded up his office, and began performing "fieldwork" in Atlantic City.

As for his graduate students, no one seems to want to discuss them, though some say they were in the office when he boarded it up.

The Adjunct

The Adjunct is in another department halfway across campus, one that really has very little to do with yours. However, because of a marginally relevant paper she published ten years ago, her name somehow became affiliated with your department, and her Web page pops up with all of the others, although her photo was taken standing in front of a different tree.

The Professor Who Wrote a Textbook

Have you heard that the Professor Who Wrote a Textbook wrote a textbook? You haven't? You absolutely have to buy it. Even though it's only fifty pages long, has no color photos, includes graphs that look like they were drawn freehand on a Macintosh in 1994, and was produced by a publishing house with the same name as the professor, it's totally the best resource out there—which is why, when you take the mandatory class he teaches during your second year, it's on the list of required reading. I mean, it's in stock at the campus bookstore, so it must be authoritative.

The Founder

Think "Strom Thurmond meets George Burns," but without the racism or the entertainment. Well, maybe a little racism.

The Founder is the only surviving member of the department's original faculty, began his research before your field was even invented (this is even true if your field is history), and, like Strom Thurmond and George Burns, is at least somewhat dead.

So out of touch that he still asks the department secretary for mimeographs—of cuneiform—the Founder still somehow maintains perfect attendance at departmental seminars and colloquia, sitting smack in the front row and shaking what's left of his head throughout the presentation. As soon as the talk ends, his black-veined hand shoots up and there is an audible exhalation of despair in the room when he declares, "I have three questions and a comment."

Students should be afraid to take him on as a mentor because, seriously, there's no guarantee he'll still be alive six years from now.

Grant Applications: Rationalizing Minutiae

Research is expensive, and money doesn't grow on trees—that is, unless they fund that proposal to breed a money tree. Money comes from grants, which are the largest and most foolishly committal statements of trust in academia. Imagine trying to get money from a bank the same way you apply for grants. "If you give me all this money," you'd tell the banker, "I'll use it for the following purposes we both know I'm lying about." And the banker would give you the money.

It's like your parents handing you ten dollars when you're a teenager. "Now, you're going to go see a movie, right? That's where this money is going?"

"*Yes*, Mom," you say, "I'm going to see a movie." Then you spend the money on crystal meth.

When writing grant applications, follow these guidelines for each required section:

Title

The title of your grant is extremely important. Remember that you'll be competing with hundreds or even thousands of other grants, so you'll want to make yours memorable. Here's an example of a good title that will really get your grantors' attention:

OMG READ THIS GRANT PROPOSAL AND PASS IT ON TO 50 OTHERS OR U WILL DIE!!! :)

Abstract

Many grant-writing books counsel you to "Tell 'em what you're gonna tell 'em, tell 'em, and then tell 'em what you told 'em." This piece of advice presumes that what you're tellin' 'em is so unclear you need to tell 'em three freaking times. But hey, whatever occupies space.

The Abstract is the first time you tell 'em. It forces you to write in twenty lines what you're about to write in twenty pages. It also makes you wonder what the point is of those twenty pages if you can summarize everything so nicely in twenty lines.

Background

Anyone who applies for multiple grants in the same field has a few "boilerplate" paragraphs that they use in the Background section of each. The more such paragraphs you incorporate, the less you have to write, so use as many as you can. That's right: The trick to writing grant applications is to do as little writing as possible.

grad student tip

Determine the time of day during which you work most efficiently. Then work at all hours of the day anyway.

Significance

Writing the Significance portion of a grant application is the only time in months that the real-world applications of your research have crossed your advisor's mind. Most academic projects have no significance—besides funding the investigation of something that happens to fascinate your advisor—so fill this section with absolute lies: "If you fund our grant to build a robot that can play badminton, um, that robot might later opt to cure cancer. It could happen."

Specific Aims

In this section, list what you hope to accomplish with the grant money. Avoid writing truths such as "We will spend most of the money on pizza." Grantors want to see what specifically you'll *produce* (which, in the case of the pizza, is poop).

If you can't think of any good Specific Aims, try to list some Nonspecific Aims:

1. We will perform research that results in a result.

2. We will generate something or learn something about something.

3. We will totally do stuff.

Collaborators

The purpose of collaborators is to commit you to working with people you've never met on a project that none of you fully comprehends. It also gives you someone to blame when nothing works.

Preliminary Results

It sounds odd, but to receive funding for work, you must first demonstrate that you can achieve relative success doing that work for free. Then...uh...you hope that the grantors will want to pay you anyway. Hmm.

Experimental Approach/Research Plan

It's difficult to devise methods for research you plan to conduct several months from now. So if you can't think of a good strategy, simply write, "Trust me."

Project Team

Your granting agency will want to know not only what work will be done, but who exactly will do the work. This is your opportunity to assemble a crack team of ragtag misfits, each with a special skill that will come in handy at exactly the right moment. ("The data are inconclusive? Luckily we've got T.J., the bony ten-year-old whiz kid, and his feisty dog Scraps.")

Budget

Most of your budget will consist of something called "overhead"—because, amazingly, when you spend money on research, other money magically disappears! Where does it go? I don't know, but isn't that a nice Lexus your advisor is driving?

References

You'll spend a bulk of your grant-writing time adding, deleting, renumbering, and panicking over the references. *What happened to reference 59? It became 58 when I removed reference 37? But then why didn't reference 41 become reference 40? Now I have to realphabetize! And why does this damn thing keep auto-formatting?*

Electronic Grant Submissions

Because we live in the digital age, when things that are actually simpler to do with paper are now forced to be digital, you can submit many grants online. This process ensures that (a) you can never tell, until you've completely submitted the application, exactly how many sections are required, and (b) everyone in the country will try simultaneously to upload their grant proposals to one overburdened, crashing website.

Extreme Makeover: Data Edition

Your advisor is in a publishin' mood, and he won't take "these are the data I actually measured" for an answer. How do you polish your results while maintaining a façade of statistical validity? Let's take one of your data sets and learn how to eliminate those unsightly blemishes, or "outliers."

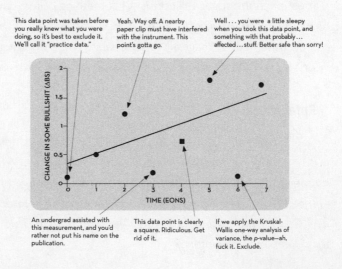

This data point was taken before you really knew what you were doing, so it's best to exclude it. We'll call it "practice data."

Yeah. Way off. A nearby paper clip must have interfered with the instrument. This point's gotta go.

Well . . . you were a little sleepy when you took this data point, and something with that probably . . . affected . . . stuff. Better safe than sorry!

An undergrad assisted with this measurement, and you'd rather not put his name on the publication.

This data point is clearly a square. Ridiculous. Get rid of it.

If we apply the Kruskal-Wallis one-way analysis of variance, the p-value—ah, fuck it. Exclude.

Y axis: CHANGE IN SOME BULLSHIT (ΔBS)
X axis: TIME (EONS)

And now the big reveal:

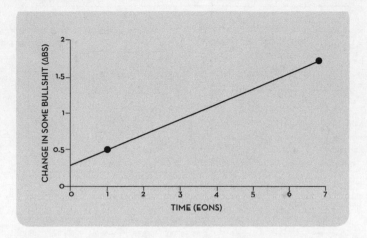

Amazing! So clean! Your fit passes *right through both data points*! Imagine that: Two data points, taken independently at two different times, are *exactly collinear*! Congratulations. Your advisor will be slightly less displeased with you.

Blind Data

In grad school, you'll have a thousand commitments, each vying for your undivided attention. So guess what: It's time to divide your attention. Divide it like a pan of brownies, and parcel out only as much as each task demands. This vital skill is called selective negligence.

When your advisor asks you to perform research, before you "try your best" or some crap like that, use this flowchart to answer the all-important question "Does this warrant genuine effort?"

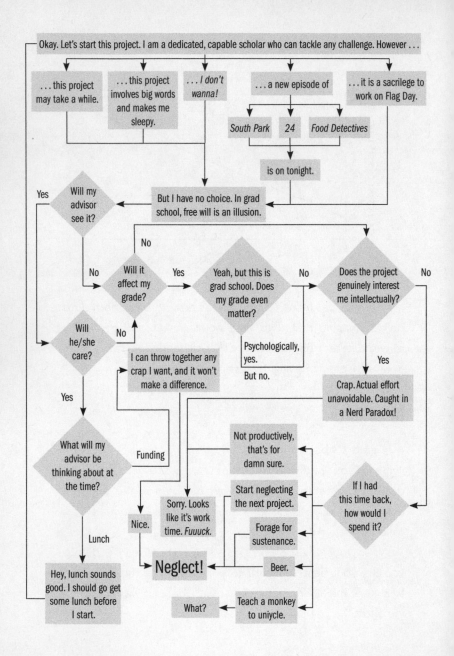

Getting Anal About Oral Exams

From their role in the Spanish Inquisition and the Salem Witch Trials to waterboarding at Guantánamo, oral exams have enjoyed a rich history. Also called "comps," "orals," or "quals," which, respectively, are short for "Completely Useless," "Oral Sex Would Be Much Better than This," and "Quaaludes May Be Necessary," your oral exam is a test unlike any other. It is a test of knowledge. It is a test of mettle. It is a test of stamina.

It is a stupid, stupid test.

Basically, a group of distinguished professors surround you, much like a group of hyenas surround a wildebeest about to take an oral exam. They start by asking about your research, with which you ought to be pretty familiar. Then they ask about your general field of study. Then related fields of study. Then unrelated fields of study. Eventually, you can actually observe them physically pulling the questions from their asses. "Why is Spain?" they'll ask. "When is Hitler?" "Balls!"*

If you know the answer to their questions, never show how comfortable and complacent you feel. Your committee will cut you off right away and move to a topic that makes you squirm. Therefore, pretend to squirm, and pretend to be as surprised as they are when you ultimately produce the right answer.

If, however, you don't know the answer, try giving one of the sample responses below. Photocopy the next page, cut out the responses along the dotted lines, and keep them in

---

* Congratulations; you found the most obscure joke in this book. Call Apogee. Say aardwolf.

your pocket. When you're stumped, pull one out and read it. Your committee will be impressed—or at least stunned long enough for you to run from the room and never see them again.

> I'm unclear on what your definition of "is" is.

> Why so much emphasis on answers? What's important is the process. And this five hundred dollars I'm about to give you. Both are important.

> Heresy!

> Please phrase your question in the form of an answer.

> The jig is up!

> If the answer I just gave is wrong, then, baby, I don't want to be right.

> An excellent question. I might ask your wife the same thing.

> I could answer that. Or, alternatively, I could show you Japanese pornography. I'll let you choose.

> It's a trick question. There are no penguins at the North Pole.

> I won't dignify that with a response.

> Does it really matter? We're all going to die someday anyway.

grad student tip

If your significant other complains that you're always off studying, lie and say you're having an affair.

Partial Arts

It's exam time, and you're ready—kind of. You've studied, drilled, and familiarized yourself with all relevant concepts—sort of. You're prepared to kick some ass (but not all ass), to pass with low-flying colors, and to give it 110 percent of the effort required to give it 70 percent.

Partial credit time, bitches.

Most exam questions have a single correct answer, but they each have many, many partially correct answers. Can't remember who wrote *Pride and Prejudice*? The answer "some woman" should at least be worth a few points. Don't know the structure of methionine? Write a C, for carbon. It's in there!

Next time you find yourself staring blankly at an exam question, try one of these techniques for getting partial credit, remembering that when you do this, you're being clever—but when an undergrad does this on a paper you have to grade, it's just annoying.

THE LONG-DISTANCE ZOOM-IN

Question: What factors influenced Molière to revise his play *Tartuffe*?

Correct Answer: Conservative factions such as the Compagnie du Saint-Sacrement viciously opposed the play, and the Archbishop of Paris threatened to excommunicate anyone who so much as read it. Thus, Molière rewrote the work as the less sardonic *L'imposteur*.

Answer That's Gotta Be Worth Partial Credit: Atoms comprise molecules, which make up substances such as paper. Paper has many uses, one of which is the application of ink thereto, a process called "writing." Those who practice writing are called "writers," of which Molière was one. In Molière's work, as in the work of many writers, individual letters combine to form cognitively recognizable subsets called "words." Molière used many words when revising *Tartuffe*, thus creating a version containing some "words" from the original and some new ones as well. The next four paragraphs will detail the history of the theater. We will begin with ancient Greece.

THE ANSWER THAT PASSIVE-AGGRESSIVELY IMPLIES THAT THE QUESTION WAS POORLY WORDED

Question: What is the density of steel?

Correct Answer: 7.8 g/cm^3

Answer That's Gotta Be Worth Partial Credit: It's a property of steel.

BEATING AROUND THE BUSH

Question: Name the two classes of stony meteorites.

Correct Answer: The two classes of stony meteorites are chondrites and achondrites.

Answer That's Gotta Be Worth Partial Credit: Oh, you know. Stuff. There are these classes and whatnot. How was your weekend?

**WRITING ABSOLUTELY, VERIFIABLY TRUE STATEMENTS THAT ARE AS
ACCURATE AS THEY ARE IRRELEVANT**

Question: Briefly summarize Jean-Baptiste Larmarck's evolutionary theory.

Correct Answer: Lamarck's evolutionary theory encompassed a "complexifying force," which relied upon the theory of spontaneous generation, and an "adaptive force," which was a precursor to modern Darwinian theory.

Answer That's Gotta Be Worth Partial Credit: Lamarck, whose first name was Jean-Baptiste, was a man. He lived for several years before he died. During his life, he formulated an evolutionary theory. This occurred prior to his death. Scholars have long referred to his evolutionary theory, and at least one assessment has been created and implemented to determine the extent of their understanding of the same. This assessment demands, "Briefly summarize Jean-Baptiste Lamarck's evolutionary theory." Such an assessment demands a response, ideally an accurate one. This response must be constructed prior to my death.

**IMPLYING THAT THE WAY THE QUESTION WILL BE GRADED MAY
DAMAGE YOUR SELF-ESTEEM***

Question: In your opinion, why does Gene shake Finny from the tree in *A Separate Peace*?

Correct Answer: Gene feels insecure about his own abilities and sees in Finny the person he will never become. This action is Gene's way of regaining control.

---

* This technique is used exclusively by entitled, sniveling little undergrads.

Answer That's Gotta Be Worth Partial Credit: In MY OPINION, Gene is really a tree-shaking alien demon from the planet Feldspar. These guys shake trees all the time. And because it's MY OPINION, you can't mark this wrong.

THE ANSWER THAT SHOWS YOU PUT A LOT OF TIME INTO STUDYING A DIFFERENT CHAPTER

Question: Are platyhelminthes classified as acoelomates? Explain.

Correct Answer: Platyhelminthes lack an internal body cavity and thus qualify as acoelomates.

Answer That's Gotta Be Worth Partial Credit: The giraffe is an ungulate mammal of the genus *Giraffa*. Its heart can weigh over twenty pounds.

THE ANSWER THAT RELIES ON A DELIBERATE, RADICAL MISINTERPRETATION

Question: Can you think of the French verb that means "to be absent"?

Correct Answer: *manquer*

Answer That's Gotta Be Worth Partial Credit: No. I cannot.

THE INEVITABLE

Question: During which geologic epoch did *Homo habilis* appear?

Correct Answer: Pliocene

Answer That's Gotta Be Worth Partial Credit: I love you.

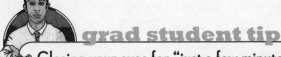

Closing your eyes for "just a few minutes" during a late-night study session never, ever works.

Academic Conferences: More Than Just a Free Hotel Room—Free Food, Too

Good news! You've discovered something extremely trivial about the world, and you've been invited to share your observations with a small room of socially awkward people paying minimal attention. That's right. You're going to an academic conference.

Academic conferences are places where scholars of all stripes, neophytes and luminaries alike, gather in one location to dress nicely and take short, seated naps. Without conferences, a scholar would never experience that magical moment of meeting someone else who has thrown his life away in the exact same pursuit. Even better, a conference may be the only event that convinces your department to pay to send you somewhere—though don't expect them to go nuts with the spending:

YOU: I thought you said you booked me a non-stop flight.

YOUR DEPARTMENT: No. We said it's a nine-stop flight.

Oh well. The point is, you're in a different town, you're interacting with new people, and you're discovering exactly how close your competitors are to scooping you.

Day 1

8:00 A.M. Wake up in hotel room (or, depending on how cheap your department is, hostel, dormitory, or packing crate).

8:15 A.M. Shower; dress crisply and conservatively. Remember, any attendee in a position of power could offer you a job—so you want to appear professional.

8:53 A.M. Arrive at conference. Stand in registration line to receive a free tote bag you'll never use outside of this conference because it says something like "Ninth International Meeting on Herpes Simplex Virus." You've never been cool, but even you have limits.

9:07 A.M. Pour a cup of coffee and enjoy a pastry from the breakfast table. Flip through the booklet of conference proceedings, circling all talks that sound interesting or relevant.

9:12 A.M. Find your own name in the proceedings and note that you are scheduled to present at 9:45 a.m. on the third day of the conference (and you've brought your laptop, so in the next day or two, you should put your talk together). Stare, flush with pride, at your name in print. It all starts here.

9:30 A.M. Keynote address begins. Take copious notes from seat at front of room. Concoct polite, incisive question for the speaker that illustrates your capacity for reason and suggests an interpretation he might have overlooked.

10:30 A.M. Keynote address ends. Raise your hand and ask your question. Speaker seems impressed but points out something *you* overlooked. Scholarly dialogue is so exciting!

11:45 A.M. Take conference-provided box lunch. Find an empty spot at a table of other grad students and enjoy the meal (except for the inevitable little container of potato salad that causes everyone to ask, "Does anyone want my potato salad?").

2:00 P.M. Sit through four consecutive presentations, paying complete attention, even when a presenter mumbles or speaks with an incomprehensibly thick accent.

5:45 P.M. On the way back to your hotel room, meet other grad students, who invite you to an evening mixer. Though you had intended to go work on your talk, you acquiesce.

8:00 P.M. Mixer begins. Strike up a conversation about your research with two grad students.

8:04 P.M. Across the room, you see *free wine.*

8:05 P.M. Commiserate with the grad students about their own programs.

8:06 P.M. Across the room, you see *free wine.*

8:07 P.M. Um …

8:08 P.M. *Free wine.*

8:09 P.M. Excuse yourself. Wait in line for ten minutes, then chug the wine immediately and get a second glass to keep you company on your next trip through the line.

9:00 P.M. Now begins the time that will live on in your memory as "a blur."

Day 2

8:00 A.M. Wake up in time for the day's first session. Immediately generate, in your head, five reasons why it would be beneficial to fall back asleep.

8:02 A.M. You can't argue with logic. Go back to sleep.

10:53 A.M. Wake up in time for the day's fourth session. Dress in whatever clothes you can find, pausing to ensure the right articles of clothing are on the corresponding parts of your body—because you want to appear professional.

11:32 A.M. Arrive at conference facility. Badger conference person- nel about where the free coffee can be found. They remind you that you missed both breakfast and the morning coffee break. Get belligerent.

11:40 A.M. Amble into the lecture hall, awkwardly carrying a sloshing mug of lukewarm coffee. Speaker, midway through his talk, glares at your interruption.

11:42 A.M. Push through a row of seated attendees to find a chair. Immediately put on mirrored sunglasses.

1:22 P.M. Wake up in time for the day's sixth session, having slept in the lecture hall through lunch.

3:15 P.M. Encounter sixth-session speaker during afternoon coffee break and ask the most intelligent question you can. She smiles and advises you to consider her department when it comes time to se- lect a graduate program. Reply that you *are* a grad student and that you're in your ninth year. Bad-mouth your own program. Cry a lot.

5:05 P.M. Locate stash of leftover wine from previous night's mixer and leftover pastries from this morning's missed breakfast. Oh baby.

5:17 P.M. Slip into your hotel room carrying five full wine bottles and a box of Danishes. Bolt the door. Your presentation is tomorrow, so you should, uh, work on it.

5:31 P.M. With a blank PowerPoint file open on your laptop to help you feel productive, alternate taking swigs of stolen Shiraz and stuffing hotel towels into your suitcase.

8:30 P.M. Take a break from procrastination to drunkenly flip through channels on the TV in your room—and oh sweet Jesus it's a *Twilight Zone* marathon!

11:19 P.M. No, William Shatner! Don't open the airplane door!

1:15 A.M. Your roommate asks you to turn off the TV, stop drinking, and please go to bed. This startles you: *All this time, I've had a roommate?*

2:02 A.M. Before losing consciousness, set your alarm for 8:15, since your talk—which you seriously plan to begin assembling in the morning—is scheduled for 9:45.

Day 3

11:08 A.M. Wake up on top of the hotel vending machine with no memory of how you arrived there.

11:19 A.M. Stumble downstairs to the conference wearing your free tote bag on your head—because you want to appear professional.

11:23 A.M. Place mouth around spigot and drink entire contents of coffee urn.

11:45 A.M. Encounter keynote speaker in hallway. Tell him his work is bullshit and his wife is hot. Throw up on his shoes.

11:50 A.M. Since you slept through your own talk, interrupt the present talk to deliver yours. Shout the current contents of your presentation across the room: "Click to add title! Click to add subtitle!"

11:55 A.M. Meet Randy, who is widely respected in his field as a hotel security guard.

11:58 A.M. Meet the rest of the field, which is actually a field. Randy has removed you from the conference and thrown you into a field.

2:20 A.M. Board flight to return home. Tell advisor you "really got your name known" at the conference. Submit receipts for reimbursement.

The Blame Game

So things aren't going well in grad school. Your classes are difficult, or your responsibilities are overwhelming, or your research is going nowhere, or your baby done left you for a grad student with access to a larger flow cytometer. But that couldn't be *your* fault, could it? Could it? *COULD IT?*

No. Of course not. The First Law of Grad School states that everything that could go wrong is someone else's fault. Whose fault, you ask? That depends on where the spinner lands. Go to the next page and give the Blame Game a spin and find out whom to bitch about today. (The spinner is really just a printed arrow, not an actual moving part—but that's the publisher's fault.)

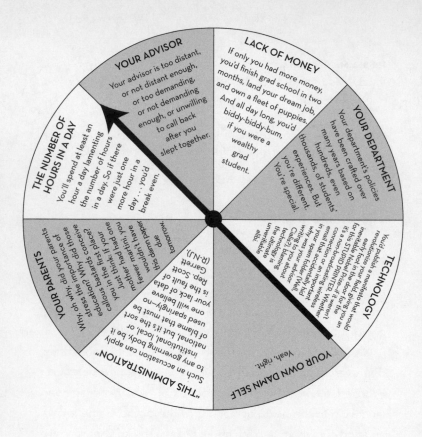

YOUR ADVISOR

Your advisor is too distant, or not distant enough, or too demanding, or not demanding enough, or unwilling to call back after you slept together.

LACK OF MONEY

If only you had more money, you'd finish grad school in two months, land your dream job, and own a fleet of puppies. And all day long, you'd biddy-biddy-bum, if you were a wealthy grad student.

YOUR DEPARTMENT

Your department's policies have been crafted over many years, even hundreds, even thousands, of students' experiences. But you're different. You're special.

TECHNOLOGY

You'd publish a manifesto revolutionize a field inevitable your foot in the door for this Nobel Prize-if the STUPID PRINTER it's a non-broadcasting you an connection email that or an important in your spam folder why was your accidentally kid writing Caliz? to your advisor technology blaming the ultimate unverifiable alibi.

YOUR OWN DAMN SELF

Yeah, right.

"THIS ADMINISTRATION"

Such an accusation can apply to any governing body, be it institutional, local, or national, but it's the sort of blame that must be used sparingly—no one will believe your lack of data is the fault of Garrett (R.-N.J.), Rep. Scott die tomorrow.

YOUR PARENTS

Why, oh why, did your parents stress the importance of those education bastards first place? Why did those callous conceive you in think: if your just had one martini, you mother wouldn't have fewer this damn paper

THE NUMBER OF HOURS IN A DAY

You'll spend at least an hour a day lamenting the number of hours in a day. So if there were just one more hour in a day . . . you'd break even.

5

Undergraduates and You

THE HAND THAT ROBS THE CRADLE

THERE'S a great line in the film *Ferris Bueller's Day Off.* (Okay, there are many great lines, but here's one.) When Ferris and his friends outwit a snooty waiter to sneak into lunch at an exclusive restaurant, the waiter sizes them up and says, before walking away, "I weep for the future."

I felt that way many times in grad school, particularly when I worked as a teaching assistant.

"But we *need* to check Facebook during the lecture!" my students would whine.

I weep for the future.

"But in high school, we were *allowed* to plagiarize!"

I weep for the future.

"I turned on the chemical safety shower because you let me get bored, and now it won't turn off."

I weep for the future. And I call the Environmental Health and Safety Department immediately.

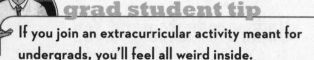

If you join an extracurricular activity meant for undergrads, you'll feel all weird inside.

To undergrads, we're the outsiders who don't belong on their campus, whose lives they don't quite comprehend, whose foreign accents they make no secret of not tolerating. To us, undergrads are the entitled little snots who have no interest in the subjects we love or the classes their parents are paying for them to sleep through.

Neither group is allowed to have sex with the other, which is more of a problem for us than for them, since on average they're hotter than we are.

What should one make of this relationship? What happens when we encounter undergrads socially? Why didn't they do this week's reading? And how do we communicate to them that serious academic papers should not, at the bottom, read, "Sent from my iPhone"? Let's learn more about academia's dominant but least evolved species, its complex motivating forces (aka "grades"), and how, together, you may covertly do the nasty.

A Little College Is a Dangerous Thing

As a teaching assistant, you'll have the pleasure of interacting with a variety of undergrads. Well, not so much "pleasure" as "obligation." After a while, you'll recognize that most undergrads, far from being the complex and unique individuals they think they are, fall into a few discrete categories:

The Athlete

Colleges are run by old people who like to watch balls being thrown well but cannot throw balls well themselves. Some young people at these colleges can throw balls well. Thus, the old people have abolished academic requirements for the ball-throwing young people so that said young people have more time to throw balls for the amusement of said old people.

Expect to receive a note from the Athlete's coach excusing him from attendance, assignments, and consequences. You might say the unfair privilege accorded to student athletes is the eight-hundred-pound gorilla in the room, but really the eight-hundred-pound gorilla in the room is the neckless behemoth who occasionally shows up and occupies an entire end of your seminar table, awakening only occasionally to drool and make long vowel sounds.

grad student tip

Having sex with an undergrad can get you suspended, expelled, or blacklisted from your department. On the other hand, you'd have sex. So there is a tradeoff.

The Absentee

Though the registrar assures you this student is in your class, you'll see her only at the midterm and final exams, when she'll casually waltz in as though she's always been attending. The Absentee will also show up on the last day of class just to fill out the end-of-semester  course evaluation, in which she'll criticize you for not being accessible.

The Extra-Credit Whore

For reasons that defy the laws of mathematics, some students believe that the points earned by "extra" credit are worth more than points earned by "credit." The Extra-Credit Whore will wait until the end of the semester—literally wait, without doing any work—and then begin begging for an extra-credit assignment. And not just any extra-credit assignment, either. An easy one. Maybe one that involves making a funny video or shoebox diorama with a friend.

The Activist

It's cute when young people think they're making a differ-ence, isn't it? The Activist has noble, unrealistic ideals ("This bake sale will cure cancer!") and strong political opinions only occasionally grounded in fact.

THE ACTIVIST: The World Bank is evil and must be stopped!

YOU: Tell me what the World Bank is.

THE ACTIVIST: Um...can I look at Wikipedia?

The flyers the Activist hangs all over campus are hilarious, too, because they can't hide the reality that the group's social function supersedes its altruism:

> ## Did you know that AIDS kills 8,000 people per day?
>
> Come to the Student AIDS Coalition meeting on Thursday at 7:30 pm in the Multipurpose Room.
>
> # *FREE PIZZA!!!*

The Legacy

When grading the Legacy's first exam, you'll notice that (a) the Legacy is as dumb as a box of frozen waffles, (b) the Legacy conveniently wrote his or her middle name on the exam, and (c) it happens to be the name of the new stadium on campus. The Legacy expects items (b) and (c) to compensate entirely for item (a). If you fear that this student could someday end up as your boss, relax: This student is your boss right now.

The Partyer

The Partyer spends every night partying and every day talking about the previous night's party. You can identify the Partyer because he arrives in class every day with a newly permanent-markered *X* on one hand and a sixty-four-ounce cup of tap water in the other. And then sleeps. And maybe throws up.

The Pledge

To some extent, all people need to feel accepted. But many undergrads need to feel accepted by a group of binge-drinking idiots whose only goal is to get into the pants of other binge-drinking idiots. While you thankfully get to miss most of this process, you do have to witness one part: the pledge period.

If students will only answer you in rhyming two-word sentences, or if they show up for class in duck costumes but won't explain why, you may initially misconstrue them as creative. Nope. They're Pledges, which means they're doing what an older idiot commanded them to do so that someday they can command the next set of younger idiots.

The Student Visa

Foreign students are absurdly respectful. In other nations, apparently, instructors command reverence, so when your students turn in an assignment, expect to see differences like this:

FOREIGN STUDENT: Pardon me, Dear Leader, but my staple has not penetrated all twenty-five pages I have authored. I am much shamed.

AMERICAN STUDENT: Yo, can I get an extension? Hey, who farted?

For all their welcome deference, though, Student Visas create a problem when it comes time to grade their work. Since English may not be their first language, your university will remind you that (a) you *cannot* grade their work the same way as that of other students, and (b) you *cannot* grade their work differently from that of other students. Somehow this dichotomy makes sense to your university, but it's the sort of logical conundrum that's been known to make robots explode.

The Canadian Student Visa

Canadian students think they're exotic because they attended International Student Orientation and don't have Social Security numbers. You can recognize Canadian Student Visas because they say things like I don't know, "I got such high marks during my grade-twelve victory lap that the Minister of Moose awarded me an igloo! Eh?"

The One Who Will Get You Expelled

The One Who Will Get You Expelled sits there, sultry and nubile, fully aware of his or her power to get you expelled. Over the course of the semester, the One Who Will Get You Expelled makes you repeatedly weigh the importance of your graduate career against the transient pleasure of turning that undergrad into an under*grab*.

Think again: Your school's deans constantly remind you that if it's true love, it can wait until the semester ends. This is because the deans lost their libidos years ago, and their genitals have long since shriveled up and dropped off like zucchini flowers. If the deans weren't sexless spoilsport eunuchs, they'd know that true love waits half an hour at the most. Like swimming after eating.

The Entitled Snowflake Who Thinks He or She Is the Center of the Universe

All of them.

Perplexed by TXT

To the professor at the front of the lecture hall, undergraduates tapping away on laptops and mobile devices look studious. But to you, the teaching assistant who stands in the back, all of their little screens are visible—and you haven't seen one pixel that's in any way related to the lecture topic.

Honestly, you wonder, why do they even come to class if they're just going to ignore the professor and text one another? Then you feel old.

As you shake your head at their goldfish-level attention spans and curse whichever misguided administrator decided to enable wireless Internet access in the classroom, you may wonder what exactly the dimwits are saying. Here's a translation of a text-message conversation between two undergrads during class:

STUDENT1> sup
Hello, colleague.

STUDENT2> hey
Good day to you as well.

STUDENT1> i h8 this class
Frustratingly, my aptitude and interests lie elsewhere.

STUDENT2> me 2
I concur. Would that I were studying the classical arts!

STUDENT1> ta is so boring
Unlikely as it seems, our attractive teaching assistant has failed to command my rapt attention. Clearly I have no one to blame but myself.

STUDENT2> lol

Your plight amuses me.

STUDENT1> dude i got so wastd last nite

You know, sending text messages in class is rude and inappropriate.

STUDENT2> i kno

Indeed. You make a fair point.

STUDENT1> u gonna git wastd 2nite?

Our rudeness ought to result in punishment.

STUDENT2> mayb

I will bake cookies for our attractive teaching assistant as a means of apology and supplication.

STUDENT1> did u git wit dat grl

Knave! It is I who should bake cookies for our attractive teaching assistant!

STUDENT2> yeh she ws ok

Let us be reasonable: We can BOTH bake cookies.

STUDENT1> lol

What a ticklishly scintillating proposal! O, such boundless cunning.

STUDENT2> dude u wanna leave

Shall we procure them on the morrow?

STUDENT1> yeh dis class sux (_(_)

No. Let us go right now, for this class sucks butt.

Paper View

Writing is the tool most academics use to obscure their research from one another. As a grad student, you'll be asked to write research papers, a task you're probably already nerdy enough to enjoy. In fact, odds are you're pretty good at it.

Undergraduates are not.

If one thousand monkeys at one thousand typewriters typed at random for one thousand years, an undergraduate would plagiarize what they wrote. (A key difference between the monkeys and the undergrads, of course, is that the monkeys would fling poop less often than the undergrads would.)

Here, then, is the difference between your papers and theirs:

Contents of the Papers You Write

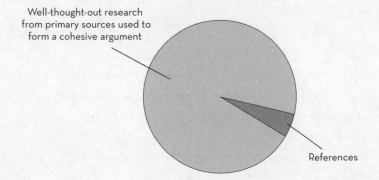

Well-thought-out research from primary sources used to form a cohesive argument

References

Contents of the Papers You Grade

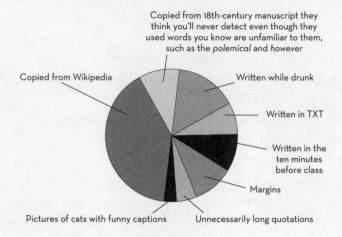

Copied from 18th-century manuscript they think you'll never detect even though they used words you know are unfamiliar to them, such as the *polemical* and *however*

Copied from Wikipedia

Written while drunk

Written in TXT

Written in the ten minutes before class

Margins

Pictures of cats with funny captions

Unnecessarily long quotations

Plagiarize This Book

Plagiarism, as you'll quickly learn if you have to grade student papers, is the theft of ideas, structure, phrasing, and your trust.

Every few years, the national news buzzes with a story about a professor on the verge of unemployment because someone discovered that three sentences from his or her paper closely match those in another professor's paper. Hearings are held, arguments rage, and the origin of each word is debated ad nauseam. In the end, a hardworking academic may resign from a multi-decade career, haunted by the gravity of a lone indiscretion.

Undergrads, on the other hand, plagiarize as often as they pee.

Undergrads believe that anything written is everyone's property to take and claim as their own—especially if it can be found on the Internet, because then they can copy and paste without even having to type it out. Undergrads plagiarize *everything*, from literary analyses to lab reports to personal essays (which you can identify if the essay begins, say, "When I grew up in nineteenth-century Poland . . ."). Undergrads even plagiarize life's daily witty remarks. Ever heard an undergrad say something relatively clever? I guarantee he or she stole the joke from *The Simpsons* or a Ben Stiller movie.

It's time to test your skills at detecting plagiarism. Can you identify the plagiarized portions of this student essay?

My Essay
By John Q. Undergrad

It was the best of times, it was the worst of times, it was the age of wisdom, it was the age of foolishness, it was the epoch of belief, it was the epoch of incredulity, it was the season of Light, it was the season of Darkness, it was the spring of hope, it was the winter of despair, we had everything before us, we had nothing before us, we were all going direct to Heaven, we were all going direct the other way—in short, the period was so far like the present period, that some of its noisiest authorities insisted on its being received, for good or for evil, in the superlative degree of comparison only.

ANSWER: None of the essay is plagiarized, because the student complained, and the student's parents threatened to sue the university, and the Dean of Negligence wants to encourage "a culture of collaborative learning," so now the student is getting an A and demanding royalties from the estate of Charles Dickens.

Gladly Shall Ye Lerne, and Gladly Chete

Professors foist the most hated tasks onto their teaching assistants, and no task is more hated than proctoring an exam. For three hours, you stroll around a lecture hall telling squirming undergrads the same thing over and over again: "I can't answer that. Sorry. I can't answer that."

And you watch for cheaters. The nice thing about stupid people cheating is that they're so bad at it—but even so, you're a little reluctant to accuse anyone. Sure, your burning sense of justice implores you to nab any student who so much as glances away from his or her paper. But blame a student wrongly, and watch out.

Crying. Indignation. Phone calls from angry parents (who always seem to be lawyers). The dreaded Ethics Committee, whose one agenda seems to be placating the angry lawyer parents. Deans and ombudspeople dressed in black robes strapping you to a table and stabbing you with number 2 pencils, while you snivel, "The student looked askance, I tell you! *She looked askance!*"

Next time, be certain. Look for the telltale signs that a student is cheating:

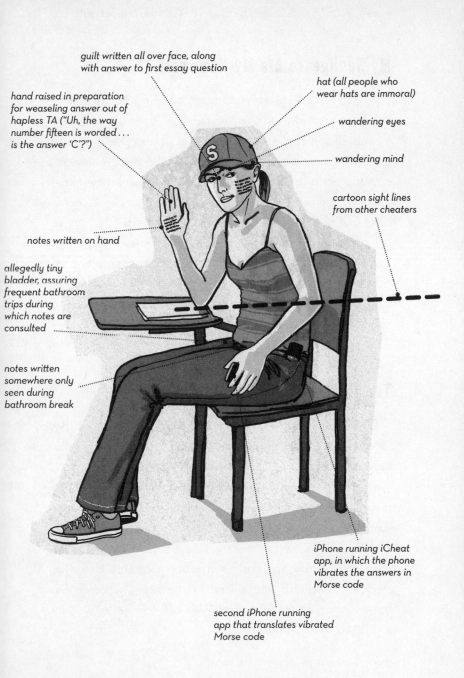

My Negligence Ate My Homework

In grad school, you strive to tease out the truth from scant evidence or murky data, especially when your advisor wants to publish something. You read the most obscure, hyperspecific academic articles on the planet to the point where you develop actual burning ire over scholars you've never met. ("Can you believe that the interpretation of Patel et al. contradicts that of Chen et al.? Those sons of bitches!")

Yours is the life of the mind, an existence in which your happiness relies upon your ability to grasp some pretty complicated shit. But can you—or *anyone*—follow the meandering logic of an undergraduate's excuse for not turning in an assignment? (See next page.)

The Testing Game

Even though they'll later claim that they failed because they "don't test well," undergrads are at their most vulnerable during an exam, making this a perfect time to fuck with them. As the test's administrators, you and the other TAs are the only relaxed people in a room full of nervous people. That's a recipe for Grad Student Fun.

With your fellow TAs, try the suggestions listed here, and give yourself the appropriate number of points based on students' reactions. At the end of the exam, whoever has the most points is the winner. We'll call the game—wait for it—Proctor and Gamble.

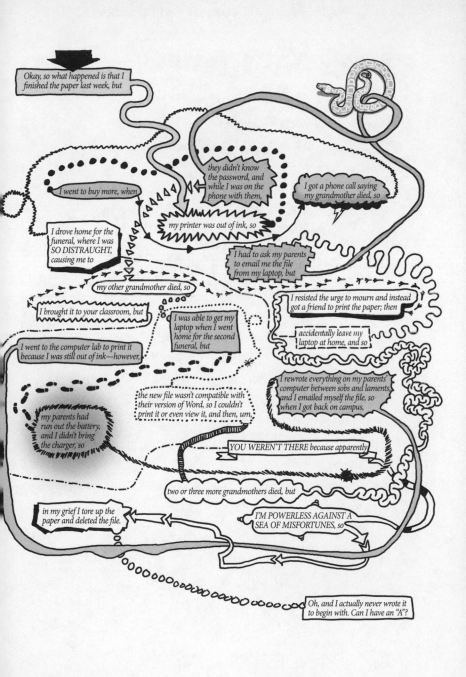

Score Card

1. Stand directly behind one student and stare at him or her, frowning, for at least fifteen minutes.

____ Student shifts positions uncomfortably (1 point)

____ Student turns around and makes pleading eye contact with you (2 points)

____ Student stands and screams, "All *right!* All *right!* I'm *cheating!*" (5 points)

2. Lean down next to a student, point to his or her exam, and, loudly enough for everyone to hear, say, "These two are correct, but this one is wrong." Then wink.

____ Student receives angry glares from other students (1 point)

____ In a desperate attempt not to be hated, student explains aloud that you two don't have a special relationship (2 points)

____ Student rewards you sexually (5 points)

____ Student rewards you sexually during the exam (10 points)

3. Look up a student's cell phone number in the student directory. Call him during the exam. When his phone rings, point at him and yell, "Get out of here!"

____ Student leaves the room (1 point)

____ Student leaves the room crying (2 points)

____ After student leaves the room crying, he answers the phone—at which point, you yell into the phone, "Get back in here!" (5 points)

4. When a student turns in her exam, look quickly through the test and laugh out loud.

____ Student asks for permission to change her answers (1 point)

____ Student sobs tears of remorse (2 points)

____ No other student turns in an exam for at least thirty minutes (5 points)

5. When about an hour of exam time remains, pick up a piece of chalk and write on the board, "10 MINUTES REMAINING."

____ Student curses out loud (1 point)

____ Student raises his hand to tell you you're wrong (2 points)

____ All students turn in their exams within ten minutes (5 points)

6. If the exam has, say, only 25 questions, pick up a piece of chalk and write on the board, "THERE IS A TYPO. PLEASE DISREGARD QUESTION 59."

____ Student frantically flips through exam pages to find question 59 (1 point)

____ Student turns exam over to look at the back (2 points)

____ Student raises her hand and says, "Um . . . there is no question 59," to which you can reply, "Wow, you're really good at disregarding" (5 points)

7. The moment the first student takes a bite of a granola bar or sips from a bottle of water, say, "I'm sorry, but there's no food allowed in this room." After he puts the snack away, take out an entire roasted chicken and proceed to eat it, along with a warm loaf of bread and a wok of mixed vegetables you sauté right there on a camping stove.

(continues . . .)

_____ Student tries to point out your hypocrisy (1 point)

_____ Student takes his food out again, staring at you to see what you'll do (2 points)

_____ Student somehow procures cheesecake and offers it to you for dessert (5 points)

8. Before distributing the real test, pass out a "joke" exam full of funny questions. Wait forty minutes while students read it, and then reveal that you gave them this fake test only to make them smile. Pass out the real exam, telling them they should get started because they've already lost forty minutes.

_____ Student demands extra time on the real exam (1 point)

_____ Student tries to enlist other students in protest (2 points)

_____ Student, not paying attention, only completes the joke exam (5 points)

9. Toward the end of the exam, with only a few students left in the room, say, "Sorry. I said 'Pencils down' five minutes ago. You've all failed."

_____ Student insists you never said, "Pencils down" (1 point)

_____ Student gets all litigious and condemns you for never putting in writing the fact that you _could_ say, "Pencils down" (2 points)

_____ Student explodes (5 points)

10. Label the first five rows "SPLASH ZONE" with no further explanation. Then, once students have sat in those rows, pee on them.

_____ Just for doing this (100 points)

On Beyond Failure!

The first time you give a student an "F," you agonize for hours. Am I ruining this young scholar's future? Am I souring him or her on learning? Have I doomed the poor soul's unborn children to poverty?

The second time you give a student an "F," you wish you could kick the grade into his or her fat, ignorant face.

It only gets worse from there.

When it does, you need a series of grades even lower than "F," for those special students for whom failure is a touch too generous. Try these:

HHH	Student exhaled loudly during class to express dissatisfaction.
I	In addition to sucking academically, student was self-centered.
L	Student made my life a living L.

MM	To compensate for failing grade, student baked me brownies. They were delicious! Student still fails.
N	Let N be an integer such that 0 < N < F.
O-	Universal donor. Student universally donated answers to lots of other students.
P	Student spent more time taking bathroom breaks than sitting in class.
Q	Student earned only ten points all semester—so I might as well give a grade that's also worth ten points (in Scrabble).
R	Student was a pirate!
T	Student was British!
T-	T minus ten seconds until student self-destructs academically.
V	Student earned a 5 percent and is also Roman.
XXX	To compensate for failing grade, student offered me sexual favors. They were delicious! Student still fails. (See also **DD**.)
Y	Student asked too many dumb questions.
ZZZ	Student slept through class.

Stages of Grief, as Portrayed by an Undergrad Begging for Half a Point on an Exam

As a rule, college students like binge drinking, holding class outside, and shirking personal responsibility. But nothing is more important to an undergrad—*nothing*—than half a point on an exam.

Even a full point is less important. Even *fifty* points. Watch undergrads ask halfheartedly for fifty points, knowing it's a long shot—but then watch them beg for half a point, convinced that their tenacity might really tip the balance. It's like watching heroin addicts beg for . . . well, heroin.

You can watch an undergrad progress through the five stages of grief:

1. **DENIAL:** "*I* didn't get the question wrong. *Physics* is wrong."

2. **ANGER:** "If you don't regrade my exam, my father will have you fired!"

3. **BARGAINING:** "How about if you let me drop this exam grade, and you just make attendance worth one hundred percent?"

4. **DEPRESSION:** "What's the point of an exam anyway?"

4½. **PASSIVE-AGGRESSIVE DEPRESSION:** "Fine. If you don't want me to succeed, *I won't*."

5. **ACCEPTANCE:** "Okay. I'll ask you again tomorrow."

We've all experienced grief. Perhaps you've lost a loved one, or had a paper rejected from a peer-reviewed journal, or arrived at a seminar just as the last doughnut vanished. But, please, the undergrad seems to be saying, have a little perspective: My half-point loss is worse than any sorrow that could befall you.

If such a tragedy afflicts any of your students, you might want to photocopy the following card, sign it, place it in an envelope, and slide it under their dorm room doors—just to let them know they're in your thoughts during this time of great misfortune.

Alternatively, you might want to tell them to shove their complaints up their asses. Your call, really.

Words cannot say
How sorry I am
To hear of your tragedy.

Know that I am here
To offer you solace
And comfort
As you grieve your unjust loss
Of half a point.

Truly yours is the burden of Sisyphus.

6

Six Degrees of Exasperation

LAW SCHOOL, BUSINESS SCHOOL,

MEDICAL SCHOOL, AND MORE

EVERY postgraduate program is its own kind of nonsensical hell.

Law school teaches us that the person who exploits the right loopholes wins. Business school embraces the wisdom of training future businesspeople to make mistakes identical to those of past businesspeople. And medical school is based on the premise that we should entrust the job of cutting our bodies to those with the least sleep.

Law school, business school, and medical school: prosecution, prosperity, and prostates. Three different types of training for three very different jobs earning three similar and ridiculously high salaries.

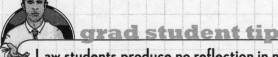

grad student tip

Law students produce no reflection in mirrors because they have no souls.

And all three make Jewish or Asian mothers very, very proud.

Lawyer, Lawyer, Pants . . . in the Foyer? (Why Are Your Pants in the Foyer?)

Imagine you're firing a missile at, say, the moon. (Don't ask why. Maybe you hate the moon. Stupid moon! I'll kick your waning, gibbous ass!)

If you change the angle of the missile's trajectory just a couple of inches, you won't notice the difference—but millions of miles away, the discrepancy will be amplified, and you'll miss the moon entirely. Then you'll have to suffer its pale glow the rest of your life, always wondering why you weren't just a little more careful with your aim.

Law school is like firing a missile at the moon. During your first year, you'll take about eight to ten classes that are nearly identical to those at law schools across the country. If you do well in these classes, you'll have a good chance during second-year fall recruitment of landing a sweet second-year summer job at a big firm. Once you've gotten your foot in the door of this firm, they'll probably ask you back during your third year, and you can parlay this experience into a cushy job for the rest of your life.

So you see, the grades you earn in a few classes during your first year of law school can decide what kind of car you'll buy someday for your kids. Shouldn't you be studying right now?

Many students begin law school because they can picture themselves shouting "Objection!" in a courtroom or reading a brief late at night and discovering the one piece of evidence that will exonerate an innocent hottie. But in reality, every lawyer's goal is to avoid being a lawyer. There are three main types of lawyers, two of which form layers of security around the third:

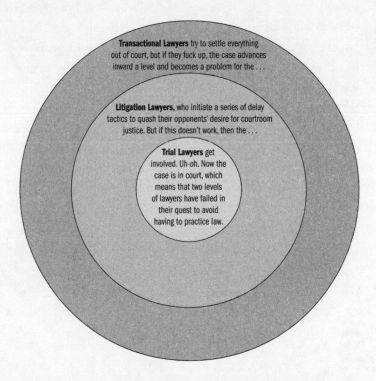

Transactional Lawyers try to settle everything out of court, but if they fuck up, the case advances inward a level and becomes a problem for the . . .

Litigation Lawyers, who initiate a series of delay tactics to quash their opponents' desire for courtroom justice. But if this doesn't work, then the . . .

Trial Lawyers get involved. Uh-oh. Now the case is in court, which means that two levels of lawyers have failed in their quest to avoid having to practice law.

That's the life of a big-firm lawyer, raking in huge piles of money in exchange for keeping your cases out of court. (Alternatively, you could eschew the huge piles of money and strive toward a job as a lawyer for the government. This is a good idea if you're a weenie.)

Taking Care of Business School

Business school is a place to study "cases," to concentrate full time on interviewing for a better job at the consulting company for which you hated working last summer, to hook up with other nerdy business students treating the experience as a chance to redo college, and to network.

Let's start with cases. A case is basically a word problem from hell, one that sucks you in with its simplicity by saying something like "The CEO was sitting at his desk, staring out the window at a blue jay in a branch of a sycamore tree" and that builds, over the course of ten pages, to a complex model of declining profit margins. Then, in class, you answer questions about the case: "What are the relevant issues?" "What course of action would you advise if you found yourself in an elevator with the CEO for thirty seconds?" In addition to wondering why the CEO would take advice from someone who shared an elevator with him for thirty seconds, you sit hoping for a question that's more your speed: "What kind of bird did the CEO stare at?"

grad student tip

If a med student overheard a business school student complaining about how much work he or she had, the med student would punch the business school student in the face.

Then there's networking, the all-purpose excuse used to rationalize anything and everything. Test your networking skills here! At the end of the day—which is a phrase you'll use every twenty minutes or so in business school—how would you justify each of the following actions?

Q: You spend a weekend in the woods doing "trust falls" and arts-and-crafts projects with your classmates as though you were still eleven years old.

A: Networking.

Q: During the busiest part of the semester, you take a trip to Aruba with several members of your class, where you drink frozen cocktails on the beach for a week and read *Us* magazine.

A: Networking.

Q: You attend your Accounting professor's mother's funeral.

A: Networking.

Q: After robbing a casino, you embark on a cocaine-fueled murder spree, capping hookers and scattering body parts across the Gobi Desert.

A: Networking.

Q: You eat a peanut butter sandwich.

A: You're hungry. And maybe the peanut butter sandwich knows a guy who knows a guy who could get you a job.

Mnemonic Plague

Medicine is all about helping people. And apparently there's no way to help people quite like rote memorization of massive, unpronounceable lists. (Every med student knows the Hippocratic oath: "Above all, memorize massive, unpronounceable lists.")

For example, you may find it's important to memorize the names of all the nerves in the wrist—because you never know when a patient might say, "Help! I have a kind of cancer that kills me only if someone doesn't name all the nerves in the wrist!"

Some say the best way to study medicine is to familiarize yourself with the basic concepts so that you can apply this knowledge to similar situations. Bullshit. While you're off using what you've learned to save someone's life, your classmate and competitor will be down the hall reciting another massive, unpronounceable list while both doctors and patients applaud her diligence.

grad student tip

Med students: Wearing your scrubs when you go out to the bar on Halloween isn't as impressive as you think.

Luckily, medical students have pioneered many memorization tricks. Choose your favorite:

Flash Cards

Flash cards are so convenient! If you write on each card one name or fact you need to memorize, all you need to do is bring a refrigerator box full of cards with you wherever you go. Then, during a particularly boring surgery, whip out your box and dig through the cards to find the series you want. Simple!

Mnemonic Device

Though there are many variations, a common mnemonic device involves using the first letter of every item in a list as the first letter of each word in an easily recalled sentence. For example, you can remember the names of all the bones in the human face (Mandible, Maxilla, Palatine, Zygomatic, Nasal, Lacrimal, Vomer, Inferior Nasal Concha) simply by remembering the following sentence: "The bones in the face are the Mandible, Maxilla, Palatine, Zygomatic, Nasal, Lacrimal, Vomer, and Inferior Nasal Concha."

Mnemonic devices are also commonly used to remember how to spell words such as *mnemonic*. Here's a good one: The word starts with *M*, and *M* stands for "Maybe you should just look elsewhere on this page, because the word is correctly spelled there."

Johnny Mnemonic Device

Why stay up all night memorizing when you can wet-wire 320 gigabytes of data *directly to your brain*?

Photographic Memory

If someone tells you, "I have a photographic memory," that's code for "I'm a dick." Sure, memorizing pages and pages of text at a single glance is useful, but even more useful—in terms of graduating from med school with your friendships intact—is pretending you can't.

Clustering

Scientific studies have shown that people remember data best if it's broken into conveniently sized clusters. Thus, if you're trying to memorize ten ways to treat a myocardial infarction, just memorize three now, three more in a few months, and promise yourself to study those last four at some point in the future.

The *Brady Bunch* Method

Remember that episode of *The Brady Bunch* in which Greg and Marcia help Jan study for her science exam? They teach her that "a primate has the size and shape of a monkey, a man, or any old ape." Jan thinks this memorization technique is neat-o! You can use it, too, provided you're trying to remember what a primate is. It doesn't really work for anything else.

Rhymes

These are fun. Rhyme the condition you're trying to diagnose with its recommended course of treatment. For example, "If the patient has cervical cancer, radiotherapy is the answer." Caution: Never recite these rhymes aloud while treating an actual patient, especially one with cervical cancer.

Association

This technique relies on the thoughts that naturally flow from one item to the next. For example, if you can't remember what to prescribe for Lyme disease, say to yourself, "*Lyme* makes me think of lemons, which make me think of the song 'Lemon Tree,' by Peter, Paul, and Mary, which makes me think of their song 'Puff the Magic Dragon,' which makes me think of the cartoon version voiced by Burgess Meredith, who was in *True Confessions* with Charles Durning, who was in *Starting Over* with Kevin Bacon, and bacon isn't healthy, so now I'm thinking about doctors, who are also called 'docs,' so I should prescribe doxycycline." By this time, the patient is dead, but that's hardly the point.

Cheating

Anatomy exams are particularly suited for writing the names of body parts directly on your body, since you'll always have it with you. Unfortunately, this technique may not work if you're studying internal medicine.

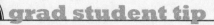

grad student tip

Imagine you paid tens of thousands of dollars to attend business school, but you didn't end up with a good job. Now imagine you bought a cheeseburger and ate it. Only one of the two actions was a wise financial decision.

ER = BS

There are many reasons to go to medical school: the ability to heal, the personal pride, the staggering salary. For most med students, however, their motivation is simple: they want to be Dr. House.

Sorry to break it to you, but House is a fictional character. His hospital is a made-up hospital. And you won't find its location, "New Jersey," on a map.

But we've all grown up watching medical melodramas, from the highly technologically advanced "computer diary" on *Doogie Howser, M.D.* to the rampant affairs and comas on *General Hospital* to the episode of *Chicago Hope* in which a six-fingered man kills Jeffrey Geiger's father. (Does anyone get that?)

Before you commit to med school, read these ways your real hospital will differ from those on television—and get yourself 10 cc's of truth, stat!

In real med school:

- The moment they meet you, patients do not tell you their life stories, and their personal conflicts do not aptly mirror your own.

- By the end of your first year, you will not likely have slept with half your colleagues.

- Most nurses do not dress like whores.

- Babies are born in the Obstetrics Ward, not haphazardly in the Obstetrics Ward Hallway or the stalled Obstetrics Ward Elevator.

- Visitors with weapons may not come and go at their leisure.

- Real hospitals average surprisingly few hostage situations per year.

- Patients typically do not stay in private hospital rooms big enough for them to wrestle with their inner demons.

- Your hospital administrator is probably not Dustin Hoffman in drag. (But if it is, then, man, that is one nutty hospital.)

- Volunteer staff cannot access any medicine they choose.

- Secretly switching two patients' charts will not automatically switch their treatments.

- The On-Call Room is not specifically designated for doctors to do it with one another.

- Scrubs are loose and functional, not form-fitting and sexy.

- No one *really* washes their hands before surgery.

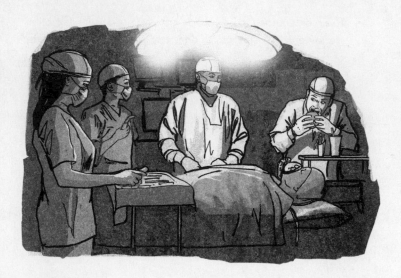

Lolgrads

Kids today and their Web-based humor. If they're not chortling at Homestar Runner's latest follies or posting embarrassing stories on FML, they're reading "tweets" or singing along to Flash-animated cartoons by someone named eBaum. Back in *my* day, we spent hours waiting for Webcrawler to load in our CompuServe window, and we liked it!*

Here's a take on the popular Lolcats site, starring grad students. (If you haven't yet seen Lolcats, go check it out right now. Your advisor isn't looking.)

And yes, you can have a cheeseburger.

---

* We didn't like it.

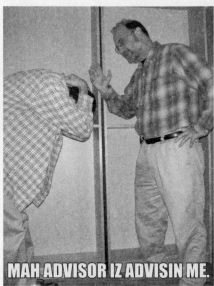

MOAR COFFEH PLZ!

I JUS REALIZD

URE HAPPIR THAN ME

I LUV MAH THESIS.

IM AKSHULLY SUFFERIN 4 REAL, AN IT NOT JOKE.

And the Rest

Besides medical school, business school, and law school, there exist a handful of other continuing education programs. If grad school gets to be too difficult, you can pursue any one of them—but don't flatter yourself into thinking they're any substitute for the rigors of grad school:

The Military

According to one recent TV commercial, enlistment in the military involves scaling canyons while slaying computer-generated dragons. Rigorous, yes, but totally fake—we won the war against the dragons years ago. In reality, rigid discipline, opposition to inquiry, and the prevalence of clean clothes make the military the antithesis of grad school.

Yoga Academies

To call a place where the instructor wears a sports bra an "academy" is, pardon the pun, a stretch. Yoga may present certain physiological difficulties, but grad students are already

grad student tip

If you join a student organization in business school, you will be given either the title "Chair" or "Co-chair."

used to bending over and grabbing their ankles—when the administration fucks them in the ass.

Culinary School

Is culinary school really less difficult than grad school? Judge for yourself:

STUDENT 1: Dude, I was up all night studying for that test on vegetables! What did you get for number six?

STUDENT 2: I got "tomato."

STUDENT 1: Aw, man! I thought it was a zucchini!

STUDENT 2: I don't think so. Zucchinis are the long green ones.

STUDENT 1: I thought cucumbers were the long green ones!

STUDENT 2: They're both long and green.

STUDENT 1: Come on! It's like they *want* us to fail!

Pottery Classes at the Y

Grad students learn the secrets of the natural world, the intricacies of the international economy, or the beauty of the printed word. Pottery students learn to move their thumbs in a certain way. Ooh.

Why is so much adult education crafts-based anyway? Is there some nationwide shortage of misshapen ceramics? Do you really need to spend six hours making a kiln-fired ashtray or a mug that's not dishwasher-safe? And don't you know what crappy gifts these make? Stop the madness! Say no to pots!

CPR Certification

You sit through one class. Your final exam takes two and a half minutes. And your diploma is the size of a business card. This is not graduate school. (Though, like many classes in which you serve as a TA, it is filled with dummies.)

Obedience School

Uh, this is for dogs.

7
Let My Pupil Go

GETTING THE FUCK OUT OF GRAD SCHOOL

TOWARD the end of my fifth year, I landed a job interview with a small biotech company. They brought me to their site and impressed me with all the cool scientific robots we can't afford in academia. As the day drew to a close, my interviewer asked the one question I dreaded.

"So," she said, "when will you graduate?"

"Well, I'm finishing my fifth year now," I said naïvely, "so if I start writing my dissertation soon, I ought to be done in just a few months."

The interviewer frowned. She snapped shut my interview folder, her expression betraying a feeling that she had wasted a perfectly good afternoon.

"We're looking for someone who can start immediately," she said. "When you have a solid defense date, call us back."

Driving back to campus after the interview, I wondered if the job would even be available in a few months, or if I would have to start searching again. As it turned out, it didn't matter. I remained in grad school nearly two more years.

Then a different deadline loomed. A few months later, my fiancée and I started planning our wedding. We wanted to make sure I'd finish school beforehand, so we set the big date far enough in the future so as to guarantee it. I could envision no sweeter moment than the wedding reception kicking off with the announcement of "*Dr.* and Mrs. Adam and Marina Ruben."

I made concrete plans. I discarded the 2005 and 2006 dissertation forms I had foolhardily obtained and picked up the 2007 forms. I told my advisor I'd like to finish a month before the wedding, and he actually gave his blessing, provided all my experiments went well. I booked a three-week honeymoon in Panama to follow the wedding.

"Dr. and Mrs." That moment would meld the end of grad school with the beginning of real life.

But as the wedding neared, I didn't seem much closer to graduation. Some experiments went well; some didn't. Bacteria stopped growing. Proteins wouldn't fold. I accidentally stabbed myself with a needle containing malaria-infected mouse blood. I wrote the introduction to my dissertation and found myself taking all day to produce one page, since each new sentence required careful rereading of a handful of references.

Then, finally, the joyous event took place in exactly the way I didn't want it to: We were pronounced grad student and wife.

And I went on that honeymoon with grad school half-tethering my attention to a different continent. From the Business Center of the Bristol Hotel in Panama City, I checked my school email account—and learned that, in my absence, a postdoc in my lab had successfully solved the structure of a protein I was working with.

"It's so beautiful!" I exclaimed to my new bride, rotating the macromolecule in space using software I secretly downloaded onto the Bristol Hotel's computer. "The inhibitor's indole ring *does* interact with the S_1 pocket. I knew it! It makes so much sense enthalpically!"

I'll never forget the look on her face. It showed . . . well, let's just say it didn't show "The S_1 pocket? Oh, rapture!"

There I sat, hunched in front of a computer, marveling at an enzyme, on my *honeymoon*—and thinking this perfectly normal. Even worse, I wondered why she wasn't as thrilled as I was.

And that's when it hit me: I needed to graduate. Now.

The Third Degree: Signs It's Time to Leave Grad School

Still here, huh? Still in grad school? Yeah, of course you are.

Do your college friends even still ask how you're doing? Or is the world sick of hearing you say, "I'm so totally completely almost done"?

Look for these signs it's time to leave grad school:

- You know the first name of at least six deans, provosts, or custodians.

- You know which water fountains on campus are the good ones.

- The younger grad students have started making jokes comparing you to Methuselah, Mike Slackenerny, or that really old Deceptacon from *Transformers: Revenge of the Fallen*.

- You have slept multiple nights in academic buildings. .

- Your first year of grad school is no more vivid in your memory than your first year of high school.

- Incoming grad students were born in a year in which you could legally vote.

- Your graduate school has automatically added you to its alumni mailing list.

- The look on your parents' faces when they tell their friends about you has changed from pride to shame.

- Your funding ran out two years ago—as did your passion for life.

- You are reading this book for legitimate advice.

Who's Who at Your High-School Reunion, and Why They All Look So Damned Happy

Your high-school reunion is a time to eat hors d'oeuvres, mingle with acquaintances you never talked to in high school, and tell each of them the same four or five facts about yourself that they could have gleaned from Facebook.

Really, you go for the food.

Because hearing your former classmates' accomplishments can feel like the most blatant encouragement to finally graduate, grad students develop a special anxiety around reunion time. While your peers have found their places in society, you still live in transition. They spend their days producing something tangible, while for you, an incisive theoretical argument *is* something tangible. They work on the twenty-third floor, and you're in twenty-third grade.

Try telling a classmate about grad school, and you'll get the pitying look that says, "You don't understand, do you? You were supposed to *do* something in the past decade." But they actually have less to covet than you'd think.

As you grit your teeth, justify why you've spent the past several years working on what's essentially a long book report, and

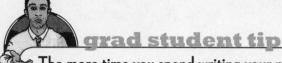

grad student tip

The more time you spend writing your prospectus, the likelier you are to figure out what the hell a prospectus is.

fill your pockets with hors d'oeuvres, hold your head (relatively) high when you mingle with the following types of people:

THE FINANCIAL CONSULTANT

Hair: Short and stationary.

Smile: Simultaneously soothing and creepy.

Refers to Employer as: Single-word proper name. ("I work at Mitchell.")

Reason Not to Envy: One of the few people who may work longer hours than you do, though he has an in-ground pool to show for it.

grad student tip

Very few schools accept a shoebox diorama in lieu of a thesis.

THE HOMEMAKER

Muffins: Delicious.

Children: Horrible, ratlike demons who bounce from the walls coated in processed sugar and Ritalin.

Daytime Soaps Watched: All.

Reason Not to Envy: You wouldn't have been happy doing this job. Seriously.

THE ORGANIZER

Most Recent Accomplishment: Organized the reunion.

Level of Evident Overexcitement in Emails: Extreme.

Is Asshole Because: Charged everyone in the class forty-five dollars for some reason.

Reason Not to Envy: Your check will bounce!

THE COUPLE

Major Accomplishments: Found true love, leased one-bedroom apartment.

Type of Dependency: Co-.

Vomit-Inducing Terms of Endearment Overheard at Reunion: Honey, Dear, Dearest, Beautiful, My Love, Hot Stuff, Pookie, Darling, Babe, Baby, Sweetie, Schweetie, Smooshums, Schmooschums, Schmooshie-Wooshie-Ooshie-Booshie.

Reason Not to Envy: Are almost certainly sick of each other.

THE HOMETOWNER

Was Born In: A small town.

Will Die In: The same small town.

Can Be Seen At: Local supermarket, high school football games, aunt's house.

Reason Not to Envy: Can be seen at local supermarket, high school football games, aunt's house.

THE HIT MAN

Refers to Employer as: Doesn't refer to employer.

Leaves: The gun.

Takes: The cannoli.

Reason Not to Envy: Unlikely to survive to twentieth reunion.

THE ONE WHO COULDN'T KEEP HER DAMN LEGS TOGETHER

Name: Almost invariably Suzy or Debbie.

Is Subject of: Gossip, scorn, drawing etched on restroom stall.

Does Not Need: Society's approval, prophylactics.

Reason Not to Envy: Whispered comments about her will supplant whispered comments about you.

THE MYSTERIOUS GUY WITH THE BEARD

Smells Like: Sheep, dishwater, mystery.

Possibly Has: Acoustic guitar, aluminum-frame backpack, improvised explosive device.

Demeanor: Eerily peaceful.

Reason Not to Envy: Uh, does anyone remember this guy? Was he in our graduating class? How did he get in here?

THE OTHER GRAD STUDENT

Reminds You: You're not special.

Beware: May engage you in a battle of misery. ("*My* advisor beats me with a rubber truncheon.")

Sad Truth: You will probably spend a majority of the reunion talking to this person.

Reason Not to Envy: Isn't it obvious?

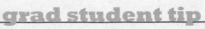

grad student tip

Become a postdoctoral fellow, and you can do this shit in your thirties, too.

Thesis Pieces

You've finally completed your (...mumble mumble...)[th] year of grad school, and as a reward for all your hard work, you get to do some more hard work! That's right: It's time to write your dissertation.

But there's no need to jump right into the scary "content" part. Let's start with something a bit easier—the acknowledgments section, a time to thank the little people who made academia somewhat more tolerable.

Think of it like Oscar night, but without the music, the stars, the glamour, the happiness, the gift bags, the montages, the attractive people, or any sense of achievement.

I would like to thank ...

- my thesis committee: for their vague and infrequent guidance;

- my thesis advisor;

- my thesis advisor's mother: Aw yeah;

- the diligent folks at Wikipedia: You sure made research easy!;

- my parents, for constantly doubting my decision: YES, I KNOW MY BROTHER BOUGHT A HOUSE;

- my significant other, for sincerely believing I had only "three months left" during the entirety of my final two and a half years;

- my department, for its outright lie about how long this shit would take;

- Nissin Food Products Co., Ltd., maker of ramen noodles; and

- of course, everyone who believed in me. So, no one.

What's Up, .doc?

Ah. Quality dissertation-writing time. You've settled in with your laptop, brewed a mug of coffee the size of a Jacuzzi, and started burning the midnight oil (because you can't afford electricity). Double-click on "Dissertation.doc" (or .docx, if you're fancy).

But wait—something's wrong! The error messages start flooding in:

File not found.
Data error reading drive C.
Sorry, but our princess is in another castle.

Your heart sinks. Your breath comes quickly. You poop a little.

And your dissertation is no more.

Every grad student has stories of that one guy who never saved a copy of his thesis, lost it in a computer crash, and then spent three weeks on the phone with customer service representatives in Bangalore trying to get it back. Some grad students have even been known to devote more hours to the post-deletion retrieval process than to the actual research that produced the document in the first place.

Don't put it off any longer. Take these important steps

to back up your dissertation so you don't get your ASCII kicked.

(Oh, and you know who those customer service representatives in Bangalore are, right? They're grad students who accidentally deleted their dissertations.)

- Save your dissertation on your hard drive. Save the entire file as a single, uneditable JPEG. This will prevent tampering. Set the resolution as high as possible—your file should be massive, unwieldy, and take at least forty-five minutes to save on what's left of your hard drive. If necessary, reformat your hard drive, and *then* save the file.

- Name the file something memorable, such as "My File" or "autoexec.bat." Change the file extension two or three times.

- Password-protect your document. Since every password can be guessed easily, choose one by shutting your eyes, pounding randomly on the keyboard, and hitting Enter. Your file will be so secure even *you* won't be able to guess the password.

- Be careful not to let the computer overheat. You can slow the processor by submerging the CPU in an ice bath.

- Copy the file onto a USB flash drive. According to manufacturers, file storage systems benefit from nearby magnets. Find the strongest magnet you can and hold it against the flash drive. If you have time, expose the drive to extreme heat and cold.

- Transfer the file to a backup tape drive. A tape drive is a storage device that maintains your data on magnetic tape. Open the tape drive, remove the tape, and affix it to the top of a flashlight. It is now microfiche.

- For added security, "burn" the file onto a blank CD. If you think this suggestion sounds like it involves fire, you're right!

- Using a standard copier, photocopy the CD. Be sure to copy both sides.

- Feed the original CD into an office shredder and microwave the pieces that emerge. This is called "encrypting" the file.

- Send the encrypted file to your own email address. There are many quick and efficient ways to send files, but the standard, preferred method is carrier pigeon—though any domesticated fowl will do.

- Many websites offer free online storage of large files. Be suspicious of these. You know who gives things away for free? Sluts.

- Just to be safe, print a copy of your dissertation on papyrus and wrap it around a glass vial of vinegar. Place it inside a stone storage vessel called a codex. The codex was invented by Dan Brown in 2003.

- Finally, and most important, lock a second printed copy inside a safe deposit box at your local bank. Your dissertation should be secure there because banks are doing awesome right now.

It's your choice. Follow these instructions and you'll keep your dissertation from "disserting" you. Otherwise, you'd better practice saying, "Thank you for calling the Support Center. May I please have the number of your warranty?"

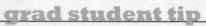

grad student tip

At graduation, do not write, "HI, MOM," on the top of your mortarboard in masking tape. Your parents don't care about you anymore.

Stretch That Dissertation! Add Fifteen to Twenty Pages Instantly Without Adding Content

With serious works of academic scholarship, quality is always better than quantity—but you have to admit, quantity is pretty damn sweet. That vellum-bound tome just feels more satisfying in your hands the more it weighs. Better for bludgeoning, too...uh, should that need arise.

For decades, undergrads have dominated the field of paper-stretching and have pioneered such useful techniques as "adding an extra space between paragraphs" and "starting the first page halfway down the first page."

Unfortunately, a majority of their tricks are easily detectable and outright dumb. "That's just the way my computer prints!" they'll whine. But triple spacing? Fourteen-point font? Really?

Morons. Transparent, sexy, drunk morons.

You need believable, sophisticated methods for taking up space. Check out this sample page from a presumably awesome dissertation, and use these tips to stretch your own! Remember, an empty sense of accomplishment is still a sense of accomplishment.

Header: Name of Chapter

SOMETHING ELSE ABOUT CHAPTER, LIKE MAYBE SECTION NAME

AND IF YOU WRITE ONE MORE THING, THAT'S THREE LINES GONE FROM EVERY PAGE! HEADERS ROCK!

Imagine that this space contains a nice, pretty picture.
Perhaps a picture of a stately elk.

Figure 1: Every figure needs a caption that explains the image in excruciating detail. You know how they say a picture is worth a thousand words? This is *exactly* where you ought to write those thousand words.[1]

This whole page has a total of one sentence of body text, suckers.

	HEADING	ANOTHER HEADING	A THIRD HEADING	GUESS
ONE CATEGORY	Data	And data	And data	And data
A DIFFERENT CATEGORY	And data	And data	And data	And data
MERGED CELLS! HOT!	And data	And data	And data	And data
	And data	And data	And data	And data
	And data	And data	And data	And data

Table 1: The table caption is the most special caption of all. In it, you completely repeat—and describe—the exact contents of the table above. How wonderfully redundant! Also, you explain obvious trends in the data that don't need to be explained and may not even exist.

Sidebar

Ain't nothin' like a sidebar to take up space. The contents don't even have to be relevant to what you're writing about.

For example, did you know that an adult panda can eat up to forty pounds of bamboo per day?

---

[1] Footnotes are used to explain your points more completely, but they don't have to. They're also a great place for irrelevant tangents. If something you've written reminds you vaguely of an anecdote, put it in a footnote![2]

[2] Or two!

Edit? Forget It

Want to calculate how long you'll spend writing your thesis? Good freaking luck. You can't.

You see, your thesis is not solely under your control. Rather, a whole group of distinguished professors works to ensure that your carefully crafted tome never ends up in vellum binding without their grubby little proofreader's marks. Between you, your advisor, and your thesis committee, there's a lot of give-and-take in the dissertation-editing process—specifically, they give you shit, and you take it.

Or, to put it differently, your thesis is "the broth," and every so often you're forced to consult too many cooks. Or—ooh, how about this one: Your thesis is like a prison bitch—subject to frequent, unwelcome input from external bodies.

In order to escape grad school, you must obtain that rarest of commodities: the editorial consensus of a bickering, ego-dominated committee.

To give you a sense of the revision process, pretend you've written a one-sentence thesis:*

The boy went to the store.

Great! You're done, right? Wrong. First you hand your thesis to your advisor for feedback. "That's it?" your advisor asks. "You need much more detail." So you rewrite your thesis, adding detail:

---

* This is absurd, as most dissertations consist of at least three or four sentences.

The small boy went to the candy store, where he bought chocolate-covered blueberries.

"Hmm," your advisor says, reading your new thesis. "The problem is that you have all that detail in there. You really should remove extraneous detail."

What? Didn't your advisor just tell you to put the detail *in*? Yes, but today's a new day. Today your advisor does not like detail. Remove most of what you've just written:

The boy went to the candy store.

Now you've learned the first lesson: Never ask for your advisor's opinion twice.

So you've got your thesis, and it matches your advisor's opinion du jour. Time to show it to your first committee member. Uh-oh! Your first committee member calls you a failure as a scholar because you didn't reference his research. Time for a rewrite:

The boy went to the candy store, as he did in Douchebag et al.

grad student tip

You'll think of time you don't spend writing your dissertation like that final scene in *Schindler's List*: "That episode of *Mythbusters* I watched—that's an hour I could have spent on my dissertation! That muffin I ate this morning—twelve minutes! *Why*?"

Your first committee member having been placated, you show the thesis to your second committee member. "Douche-bag?" cries your second committee member, glaring at you incredulously. "You're citing Professor Douchebag? He's completely irrelevant! If you don't remove your reference to Douchebag, I'll never approve your thesis."

Okay. Douchebag disappears. Behold:

The boy went to the candy store, as has been seen previously.

Oblique enough? Maybe. But guess what: now your third committee member is unhappy. "In *my* field," she tells you, "we focus on the journey itself."

"Yes," you reply, "but my dissertation isn't about your field. It's about my field."

Nice try. But your third committee member cannot fathom a world in which all research doesn't relate to her field. Thus:

The boy walked up Main Street and made a right on Third Avenue to get to the candy store, as has been seen previously.

Your fourth committee member is the fun one. Unfortunately, *fun* doesn't mean "fun." It means, "Ooh! I've got a fun idea for something you can add to your thesis!" Such ideas are rarely fun and cost you assloads of extra time.

"Rewrite it as lyrical Irish narrative free verse!" squeals the committee member, clearly having so *much fun* with your thesis. Okay:

The boy walked up Main Street and made a right on Third Avenue, diddle-hi, diddle-ho, to get to the candy store, as has been seen previously, hie-dee-dee, hie-dee-doo.

Time for the last step in the process: Show the finished product, once more, to your advisor.

Your advisor reads your thesis. You wait in judgment. Did you properly balance your advisor's and committee members' whims? Did you strike the rare and difficult balance between each of their narcissistic attempts to recast your thesis in their own style? Is your thesis acceptable?

Your advisor emerges from his office after three months and hands you your thesis with a single written comment: "No."

Aha. A new game! The process has evolved from "Do what I say" to "Guess what I'm thinking." So you rewrite:

The boy . . . um . . . walked . . . or maybe he didn't . . . and the store . . . blueberries . . . hie-dee-doo.

"Excellent!" says your advisor. "I completely approve! However, in the two years it's taken you to edit your thesis, the field has changed. Everyone already knows that the boy went to the store. You need a new topic."

The girl jumped rope.

"But," you plead meekly, "my life—"

"Just let me know when you're finished," interrupts your advisor, "and I'll be glad to angrily provide comments. Oh, and make sure you've put in lots of detail."

Nothing to Approve

Behold the dreaded Thesis Form, the single sheet of paper that spells out your fate. While your thesis committee takes half an hour to review and discuss your multi-year struggle, the committee head has this form, a pen, and more power than you're comfortable with.

Admit it. Your sphincter contracts a bit when you see this form, doesn't it?

Student Name: _____ Date Thesis Submitted: _____

Yes No

O O Student completed required course work.

O O Student performed adequate independent research.

O O Zest for life hammered out of student.

O O Student's health deteriorated the requisite amount.

O O Dissertation is thick, obscure, and innocuous.

O O Manuscript details meet arbitrary standards I established this morning and told only my dog.

O O Student left $500 in small, unmarked bills in my department mailbox.

O O Student left $500 in large, marked bills in my rival's department mailbox.

O O Academic job market shitty.

O O Stars aligned.

○ ○ Student realized he/she is being kept here only as a source of cheap labor.

○ ○ It is less work for me to approve this thesis than to disapprove it.

○ ○ Student promised me a night of passion and a lifetime of discretion.

Therefore, on this _____ day of _____, we officially (approve / disapprove) this student's graduation (unanimously / with much unnecessary bickering). We offer our sincere (congratulations / condolences). Student must now get very drunk to (celebrate / mourn).

Signatures of committee members who approve student's graduation:

_____

Signatures of committee members who disapprove student's graduation, despite student having obeyed their instructions exactly:

_____

Doodle distractedly in this space:

Certificate of Depreciation

Step 1

Step 21

Congratulations! You've graduated! (Well, let's pretend.)

You've just sat through a commencement ceremony in the blistering sun (the perfect time to wear a heavy black velvet robe), listened to a college wind ensemble's forty-minute rendition of "Pomp and Circumstance," and texted your parents to let them know where you were sitting. Now, for all your years of effort, you've earned (a) a piece of paper and (b) the ability to truthfully refer to that piece of paper on your résumé.

Then, as months pass, you realize that if your diploma is good for something, that *something* sure as hell isn't getting a job.

What good *is* an advanced degree, then? What *can* you do with your diploma?

- Prop up the short leg of your coffee table, provided it's only one-one thousandth of an inch short.

- Wrap a small present—once.

- Show it to everyone at the singles bar (if you truly, truly hate getting laid).

- Crumple it into a ball and have your classmates do the same. Diploma fight!

- Cut out the letters, paste them on a blank sheet of paper, and anonymously send your former thesis advisor...uh...let's say, feedback.

- Earn three more degrees and have a handy set of disposable placemats.

- Frame the evidence of your erudition and hang it... upside-down! O delicious irony!

- Shred it to make bedding for a very special hamster.

- If your degree is a PhD, cross out "PhD" and write "Master's," so that you can actually get a practical job.

- Photocopy it, and mail it to that high-school teacher who said you'd never amount to anything. It's your way of saying, "See? You were *wrong*. I *did* amount to something. I'm a person who can afford a *postage stamp*."

- If you find you miss the daily pain and nagging annoyance of grad school, give yourself a paper cut.

- Wallpaper every room in the only house you can afford. (You'll still have leftover paper.)

Career Ends

Ask children what they want to be when they grow up, and you'll get answers that are as cute as they are unlikely—yet we still tell kids that they can be anything they want to be, and they believe us. Crane operator? Sure. Professional baseball player? Why not? Fire-breathing princess? Uh, okay.

By the time you enter college, the phrase "when I grow up" gets a bit awkward. Technically, you've already grown up—you're just taking four years to prepare yourself for your dream career—so "when I grow up" might just mean "next June."

Spoken in grad school, "when I grow up" is simply depressing, because:

1. Your career choice has gotten very specific and very boring. ("Someday I want to be a visiting lecturer in an expository writing program!")

2. You're thirty-two freaking years old. Don't let your kids hear you talk that way.

Now that you've nearly grown up, it's time to decide on a career. As you can see from the following list of potential jobs, the possibilities are limitless, except in the sense that they're extremely limited. Pick your favorite, and go fantasize about the career you'll begin "when you're middle-aged and broke."

Professor

The academic route has two stages: First you're an assistant professor, whose job is to get tenure; then you become an associate professor, whose job is to have tenure. Sound like a satisfying life? If you're a fan of cruel irony, staying in academia is a good way to perpetuate the accursed cycle that enslaved you for so many years. That way, when people ask what you do for a living, you can happily declare, "I'm part of the problem!"

Captain of Industry

If your degree is in science or engineering, you have the option of leaving higher education to work in industry—or, as the snooty academics call it, "going to the Dark Side." This is an allusion to *Star Wars* and would be accurate—if those on the Dark Side worked shorter hours, got paid more, and contributed meaningfully to society.

Strange, Oblivious Hermit

Imagine yourself unshaven, stoop-shouldered, and babbling incomprehensibly—like a grad student, squared. As popularized by that guy who lived in Val Kilmer's closet in *Real Genius*, this is the career choice of many physicists and mathematicians, who proudly declare themselves "pre-hermit." If you've ever thought, "Yeah, I could see spending a decade in a garage full of Mountain Dew cans and mail-order centrifuges," take one last look at the sunshine, grab a final shower, then get to work. The world awaits your brilliance.

High-School Teacher with an Advanced Degree

Maybe you have visions of being that one influential educator, speaking articulately with warm frankness and smiling while crinkling your eyes, like Robin Williams in *Dead Poets Society*, or Robin Williams in any other movie. Or maybe you have visions of the slight pay increase your degree will earn you (if you work for fifty years, it will financially compensate you for your decision to go to grad school!). But, really, you just don't want to suffer through years of the tenure process before you get to order people around in the classroom.

Professional Student

If you're dedicated, efficient, and truly, truly fucked in the head, you may choose to pursue an additional degree. Perhaps you think your PhD is a nice precursor to law school, or perhaps you have a master's, but you want a different kind of master's. It's more likely, though, that you're just scared of the real world. Either that or you honestly want to become a medical patent attorney and civil engineer who writes creatively about early existentialist philosophy—in Sanskrit.

Someone Who Squandered Something Very Precious

Once you earn an advanced degree, everyone's expectations of you rise, revealing a previously inaccessible swath of potential disappointment. If, say, you never finished high school, your loved ones will be proud if you end up as an airport shuttle driver. But bag an unused degree, and suddenly it's the first half of every sentence about you: "That's Uncle Dave. He actually has a PhD in chemistry, but now he lives in that godawful fishing colony. I think he traps eels or something. Such a waste."

Haven't Thought About It

Uh-oh.

Epilogue

GRAD school is a world of shit. It just is. You know this.

You work a job with hours that bleed into and subsume your free time. You earn the leanest praise and mediate the pettiest disputes. You're paid very little, or nothing at all, or—big fun!—*you* pay *them*. True, there are moments of real personal discovery, but also tedium, repetition, seminars, and repetition. Even if you vehemently love your subject—and to justify your stupid, stupid decision, you'd better—the day-to-day drudgery can quickly crush your initial idealism.

As each day brings more doubt and less progress, you get caught in grad school's academic undertow, and even when you notice what's going on, your natural response is not to act, but to complain.

Please allow this book to offer one piece of serious advice (don't worry, this is the only one): Take control.

Decide that enough is enough. Stop waiting for your advisor to guide your work—write a paper using your own brain and slap it down on his or her desk. Study—really, actually *study*—what it is you're studying. Realize that you can't include *everything* in your thesis, and drop your lofty and unrealistic plan to transform the field. You won't. Plan what you need to do to graduate, write it down, sit with the person whose approval you need, and work up a timeline. Seek out interesting conferences, and if your department won't pay for you to attend them, search for outside sponsorship. (You have the

freaking Internet, for crying out loud.) Actively pursue your own intellectual goals, because—and it's so easy to forget this—that's why you're here.

Can't find the motivation to work today? Tough shit. It's like a snow day: Every day off you give yourself makes you feel good that day, but it's one more day you'll have to make up in June when you *really* want to be out of school.

It's possible that many graduate programs *want* you to get depressed, say "Fuck it," and take charge of your own destiny. They may consider this part of your necessary struggle. Well, so be it. Wait no longer. Take charge now.

And get on with your stupid, stupid career.

AN EPILOGUE *and* an afterword? Really?

No.

ACKNOWLEDGMENTS

DOES anyone actually read the acknowledgments who isn't mentioned in them? Don't feel obligated.

First and foremost, I'd like to thank my agent, Laurie Abkemeier, and my editors at Broadway, Laura Swerdloff and Hallie Falquet. You all said yes when everyone else said, "Grad students are poor and won't buy books."

I am quite grateful to my illustrator and former college roommate, Darren Philip, for his outstanding contributions and for not even flinching when I said, "I need you to draw a badminton-playing robot being awarded the Nobel Prize for Medicine." (I love that picture. Go look at it again. It's hilarious.)

Many thanks also go to the current and former students who gave me valuable advice about their postgraduate experiences: Rachel Ruben, Lee Hadbavny, Abby Sheffer, Eric Huang, Susan Merino, Gene Bialczak, and Hannah Bascom.

It was fascinating to learn how our experiences differed, and horrifying to learn how they were similar.

I'd also like to thank everyone who reluctantly agreed to appear in the Lolgrads photos: Sam Leachman, Chuck Na, Erin Vaughn, Jayson Hyun, Marina Koestler Ruben, Dan Koestler, "evil advisor" Dr. Bob Koestler, and Pico the Cat.

Even bigger thanks go to those who read drafts of the book: my parents—Jeff and Gina Ruben—and especially my wife, Marina, whose edits were so thorough that she even caught an apostrophe—in nine-point type—facing the wrong way. (She probably doesn't like the fact that there are four em dashes in that last sentence, either, but that's life.)

And of course I'm going to do the cheesy thing and thank *you*, the purchaser of this book. I hope it made your burden a little more bearable, and if not, you can probably sell it back to the campus bookstore for fifty cents or something.